Always & Forever, Love

Success Stories of Marriages 20+ Years Strong

Written by : Otis G. Sanders

7thSon Productions, LLC
P.O. Box 9061
Inglewood, CA 90305
http://7thsonproductions.org

First published by 7thSon Productions, LLC, 2011

Paperback ISBN: 978-0-9830193-0-5

Library of Congress Control Number: 2011912912

Printed in the United States of America by Sumi Printing, Carson, California

Dedication

This book is dedicated to my wife Freda. Thank you for being there during this and all the other projects I have on my list. You make it easier for me to be an artist, father, and husband by realizing and understanding that my thoughts and ideas sometimes take me places I have to travel alone.

I love you, Always & ForEver.

Acknowledgments

I'd first like to give thanks to God and all seven of my Guardian Angels for watching over me each and every day of my life and keeping me on the path that has been chosen for me. It is my thought that our path in life has already been chosen for us, our job is to find that path and follow it to its end.

I owe many thanks to my long time friends, Floyd & Carla Williams. They were with me at the inception of this idea and have given much advice, information, and knowledge on the subject of marriage and publishing. Since they've been married for more than 20 years themselves, they were the first couple I interviewed for this project.

Thank you Gennie, for finding all the couples in the book from Atmore, Alabama. And thanks to my brother Lindsey for finding the oldest couple with the longest standing, successful and happy marriage in the book, Willie and Eliza James of Stockton, Alabama.

Paula Clagon worked her magic building the website for the book. Matthew Brown, thanks for lending your Photoshop expertise on the website images and the promotional postcard.

Cynthia Mitchell, thank you for all you did to get the ball rolling with the design of the book cover.

Endre Yancey, thank you for doing all that you do, websites, design, logos, laying out this book, the e-book, being a computer tech and much more! You've done everything I've asked (even if you didn't know how to do it) and a lot of things I didn't ask, but needed. I couldn't have done it without you!

Shelby Benton, thank you for the interviews, offering marketing suggestions, passing the word about the book, and your excitement all along the journey.

Laura Cook, thank you for adding your creative and thoughtful words to the book in the form of poetry.

The words I've written for this publication were rearranged, moved and changed to make for a more understandable read by my editor, Flo Jenkins. Thank you so very much for all you've done.

Laurie Brown, I can't thank you enough for taking time out of your busy schedule to read and make suggestions for the interviews with a fresh pair of eyes.

To Anderson Pratt, who's more family than a friend, thank you for getting involved and producing the photo shoot of your parents, Walter and Thelma Pratt. The shoot would not have happened without the help and complete attention of Debbie Pratt and Nick. Thank you both for being and doing everything I needed.

I cannot forget two people who have been such a great support to me since we met 30 years ago. They both requested to remain anonymous. They say, *"Our greatest joy comes from the fact that you continue to create great images."* They both have a great love for photography and a great appreciation for photgraphers and artists in general. They care as much if not more about artists on a personal level and what makes them work as they do for their art. This book would not have been possible without their philanthropic generosity. Thanks for always being there for me, and for believing in this book as much as I believe, and all the other projects over the years.

I'd like to give a special thanks to James Fugate & Thomas Hamilton of EsoWon Books in Leimert Park, Los Angeles, California for guiding me in all areas of book publishing, marketing and selling.

Pam Perry, the PR Coach of Ministry Marketing Solutions and Steve and Bill Harrison of Radio-TV Interview Report (RTIR), thank you guys so much for all the great info regarding book marketing.

Kamau Ramsey, thanks for picking up the phone (past your bed time) when I called to ask yet another question about publishing.

Thank you, Taina Johnson, Carl Pruitt, Cassandra Bell, Dale Birdsong, Kevin Brown, and Shirley Robinson for all of your support, help, and advice along the way.

Thank you to Sumi Printing owners Roland & Michel Sumi for working the numbers making it possible to produce a stunning book. And many thanks to Mr. Peter Summers, the key account executive at Sumi Printing, for walking me through the whole printing process.

DJ Robinson, Sheila Booker-Campbell, Lena McIntyre, Myne Whitman, James (Maceo) Rogers, David McKnight, Gerry King, Tracy Lamonica, James Owens, Keith Sherins, Trutina Maria Sowell, Teresa Sanders, Verla Saylor, Prentice Hill, Reginald Saunders, Patricia Titus, Irene Odebunmi, Chris & Laurie Brown, Arzell Dupree, Valencia Myers-Benjamin, Debra Phifer, Roosevelt Sanders, Juan Lopez, Larry Hawley, Virginia Hill, Jennifer Durham, Terry & Deena Green, Tereska Hampton, Troy Harrison, Mrs. McCaleb, Lurlean Towns (moms), and Andrey & Lisa Wilkins, thank you all for believing in me enough to purchase pre-published copies of this book months in advance of publishing.

To all the couples that participated in this project, without the generous input of your time, energy and insight, this book would not have happened. Thank you so very much!

Table Of Contents

Introduction

As I ponder the idea that a literary presentation will be honoring couples that have sustained their marriages for better than twenty years, I smile! Marriages that last better than a quarter of a century are special. But marriages that sustain for that duration going into the new millennium are nearly a miracle. Divorce has a major impact on the health and wealth of our current society. This nation, many of the states, and the metropolitan cities within those states suffer greatly when divorce is the option. Overall, divorce has contributed to the state of today's poverty.

While the concept of marriage has become a secondary cultural or social event, married couples are currently a minority in the national census. This leads me to reflect on the past times of Americans when even marriage amongst minorities had greater numbers and successes. Households with children

of single parents was significantly small and nearly non-existent compared to today's numbers. The rate of divorce was less than fifty percent. Some recent statistics note that in 1960 and before, divorce was only 24 percent. Parents that were married at the time of their child's birth was 92 percent. The current percentage has expanded to more than 69 percent and will exceed 72 percent by the year 2010.

College and Senior High School students who were polled about marriage, significantly (96%) believe in marriage and expressed that some day they will be married. Unfortunately, however, marriage vs. cohabitation statistics among young adults show cohabitation is leading. Granted, the media in general, including television and the movies do not provide a positive outlook on the reality of marriage, so it is essential to showcase to the world, and espe-

cially Americans, that marriage can last a life time. And demonstrating it with regular people of various communities and diverse walks of life is even more important. Long lasting marriages may not always equate to long lasting love, but it is a greater variable than the alternatives of divorce, abandonment, or lengthy separations. As my wife, Sonja, and I have celebrated thirty-eight years of marriage, we are proud to be a part of this effort. I feel excitement for this book, *Always & Forever, Love*—authored by Otis G. Sanders. We understand the painstaking challenges of a long lasting marriage and the hard work that accompanies long lasting love. I believe this publication can make a powerful impact on uplifting and rekindling the institution of marriage in America by ceremoniously highlighting married couples; and by presenting a refreshing, positive spin on something historically so sweet and special, but

which for over the last forty years has become unceremonious trivial and unpopular, (albeit) negative in the eyes of so many.

"Marriage is a vessel for living love" as the songwriter lyrically describes it. I believe that this book pays homage and serves as a photo literary "hall of fame." It's serving as a modern day almanac for God's greatly ordained blueprint for man and woman to keep love, until that time they mortally part. The importance of its publication is a footnote on marriage as a vessel for those who genuinely love one another. May this inspire those who choose marriage for themselves yesterday, today, and the future, proving that marriage can last a life time, and it can sustain itself and all the beauty that's brought to it.

La Grande E. Mason, Jr., Ph.D.
CEO/Executive Director
Los Angeles Healthy Marriage,
Family & Community Coalition

Author's Note

What is that thing or set of circumstances that keep married couples together for 20 years or more? And how are they able to remain in love after being together for so long through the ups and downs of marriage? What does it take? Why are some successful and others are not? What is the common thread, or glue, that has kept couples together? These and other questions were the driving forces that started the process that led to this book.

Growing up, I remember watching my grandmother (Big Momma) and grandfather interact. I knew they had been married for many years (55 in all), and they seemed to be so perfect together, even during the times they argued or had disagreements. There were struggles, but the glue that stuck them together was their desire to be together in spite of them. There were times when my grandmother was in the kitchen cooking dinner and my grandfather, sitting at the dining table would yell out, "Let's get some food on this table!" Meanwhile, in the kitchen, my grandmother pretended she could not hear what he said and continued to prepare dinner; but at the same time I could see her mouth move as if she was saying something quietly so he wouldn't hear her. She wore a hearing aid, but I think she had selective hearing, especially when it came to hearing what my grandfather had to say. After all was said and

done, my grandfather got his food on the table, and we all sat together to have dinner and everything was great. The very next day the same thing would happen all over again as if it was scripted.

It seemed to me that over the many years they had been together, through 13 children and everything else that went on in their house, they had settled into a routine that they both could live with. My grandparents were together until they were no longer able to take care of themselves. In their old age, when they could no longer take care of themselves, they were then taken (separately) to live with their children, then to nursing homes. These were the only times I remember when they were apart in all the years of their marriage. I didn't know it then, but there was a lot to learn from watching my grandparents. I'm sure it took years to find the music they danced to, but their dance lasted 55 years.

The information presented by the couples in this book along with the photographs are just a small glimpse into their 20 + years of marriage. It's not possible to include on one page the many varied life experiences, challenges, accomplishments and failures these couples have witnessed and been a part of.

God/Spirituality, Respect, Communication, Forgiveness, Love, Trust and Togetherness were some of the words used most by each of the couples I interviewed to help explain their success in marriage, though not always in that order. Having a wide age and ethnic range of participants in this book is my attempt to show that the ingredients in the glue that hold and keep a marriage together is the same for all races and ages, without regard to their location, education and occupation.

Some of the participants in this book from my hometown of Atmore, Alabama have known me for most of my life. Others knew me and my family; some are friends, relatives of friends, and friends of friends and family. I chose these couples to participate because I wanted to see how close or far I was away from successful marriages. After all is said and done, it is my desire to demonstrate that, although the divorce rate is indeed high, there are a great number of couples that remain happily married and in love for many years.

Picture taking

In the hands of this artist-lover, the camera becomes an apparatus of "picture-giving" –– giving the beauty of these lovely couples to themselves and to the world. Above the wasteland of fractured, broken relationships, media scandals and tabloid divorces, these smiles rise like an eternal honeymoon. The sweetness of their faces gets all in our faces, challenging us to be better. Each of their stories testifies of commitment; the power to make the marriage work overrides every circumstance. Monarchs, they bear the stamp of royalty. All the wedding planners, seamstresses, haberdashers, caterers or priests in the world cannot manufacture the strong character of these individuals. Nor can it be purchased. One can but wonder how the butterfly makes a journey of a thousand miles on such frail, powdery wings!

Matthew, poet in exile

Survival: The 'Make Up'

how many times has it cross our minds
that we just might not survive this time

and how many deaths
must we die to self
before we cast vain pride aside

if you are my treasure
then your value out measures
my need
or my urge
to be right

I will pick up the weapon
of love I'm confessin'

…some battles best won, less the fight

Always & ForEver, Love

20 to 35 Years

Yearnings Of Our Newness

memories
kiss the nape of my neck
with candle lit moments of our own wicks
ignited excitement of
finally i get to hold you again
…8 hrs can seem so long

©ImmoBme az.i.B.we
Jan. 15, 2011

Richard and Trish have been married 20 years, but knew each other for almost as long before they wed. They met in 1974 when Richard was working in Torrance at the city's Friday night dances for grade school students. During intermission, the students were to learn gymnastics. Trish was one of the instructors. After the lessons, they all went out for pizza. The two exchanged phone numbers, but they didn't communicate until about a year later.

Richard was attending the Art Center College of Design in Pasadena and called Trish to model for him after he was given a photo assignment. They completed the assignment and later he shared his photos with Trish, who was attending Long Beach State finishing her degree in Fine Art, Drawing and Painting, in addition to teaching gymnastics.

The couple began dating about 2 years later, after Richard was given another assignment to photograph a pair of shoes that were about a size four. The only person that Richard knew with feet that might fit the shoes was Trish, so he gave her a call. The photo shoot was successful, and afterwards, as he was taking Trish home, he decided to stop for dinner. During dinner, Trish played a trick on Richard; as a result, he decided Trish was a lot of fun to be around. The next years brought them closer as they spent time getting to know each other. They went sailing and traveling--basically doing interesting things together and with close friends.

"We had to be really sure before we said we would get married." —Richard

During their years of dating, marriage was never a big concern for either of them, because they were having fun just enjoying each other's company. They have been married twice (unofficially). The first time was when they went hot air ballooning. After completing their flight, they were given a certificate that listed them as "husband and wife." The second time occurred on a sailing trip to Catalina. Their friends onboard decided they should be married, and thereby actually wrote their vows,

made a veil, prepared a bouquet from paper, and "married" them on the return trip. The skipper of the boat was said to have authority to perform ceremonies at sea.

"Trish is my best friend ever!" —Richard

On October 28, 1991, Richard and Trish decided to get married on a weekend trip to Big Bear Lake. Richard had already bought Trish a ring. As they talked about the idea of getting married, he thought they would have to do it another time, because he didn't think Trish had a ring for him. Some time previously, however, Richard's parents had sent Trish Richard's grandfather's wedding ring. Because they had spent so much time on the water sailing, they decided that's where they should be married, on water. They arranged to be married in the middle of Big Bear Lake on a pontoon boat with only them present, along with the minister who performed the ceremony, and the owner/captain of the pontoon boat.

Richard recalled, "From the very second I said, 'I Do,' I felt different. After being together all those years and living together, I felt like we were a partnership, thick or thin--we were a team." Trish explained, "Our marriage is successful because we get along really well; we don't fight-- but that's not to say we don't get upset with each other, but nothing lingers. We've realized that we love each other even over the differences we might have.

"What brought us together initially is still what keeps us together: we just have fun together. We feel like we're a team working together with the same kind of values in regards to family, friends, and personal integrity. We function well together, as we have more similarities than differences."

Richard & Trish Ruthsatz - Torrance, California
Married 20 Years - Anniversary: October 28, 1991

Ray & Cindy Reding - Redondo Beach, California

Married 21 Years - Anniversary: February 10, 1990

Cindy and Ray were students of photography at the Art Center College of Design in Pasadena, California when they met. They were in the same design class when Cindy dropped her pen and was frantically looking for it. Ray saw her looking for it when he said impatiently, "The Pen is gone!" Ray didn't like Cindy in the beginning partly because he viewed her as competition in class, and also because he sensed something different about her since she was always cheerful and friendly to everyone.

Almost a year later, during finals, Cindy called a mutual friend of theirs for help to complete her photography assignments. Ray happened to be at this friend's place, so they both went to help Cindy complete her assignments. After finishing, Cindy and Ray went out for a drink and spent some time alone. Ray remembers seeing a photo project Cindy did for class. It made him look at her in a whole new light, because he saw how honest, deep, thoughtful, and insightful she was. That was the beginning of their relationship. Both are very creative people, interested in photography, art and self expression.

After leaving college, they went into business together, setting up a photography studio. Ray and Cindy were in business and living together for 11 years before they were married, but during those 11 years, there was at least one year that they were not together. Ray says, "I just sat by the phone waiting for it to ring." Cindy remembers her mother initiating a divorce from her father when she really wanted them to stay together. She used that instance to remind her that losing Ray over a small misunderstanding was not worth it.

"Ray has so much respect for me as a person and as an artist." —Cindy

What's special about the relationship Ray and Cindy had together from the beginning is that they were each living their dreams of being professional photographers, expressing creatively their ideas together, separately, for clients, to each other, and through each other.

Ray and Cindy say that communication, compromise, keeping themselves happy, healthy, and being able to look at one's own faults in the same way as they see their spouse's faults, has gone a long way in helping them maintain a successful marriage.

"If you lose yourself, you lose everything." —Ray

One of the most challenging obstacles they've had to live with, adapt to, and overcome in their marriage is the closure of their studio. They had to separate their working and artistic lives, and work apart from one another, which meant that they would no longer be able to strive towards the same goal of operating a photography business together. Now they have to survive life working separately. That might not be such a major thing for most couples who have not worked together closely or shared 18 years in the same creative profession and business. There was quite a bit of strain on the marriage because they went from being together all day every day to seeing each other only in the evening after a long hard day, doing work that was not emotionally fulfilling and unrewarding.

Since the closure of the studio, Ray said, "We've had to constantly check ourselves, adapt, and grow. We've found ourselves in positions that were constantly testing us and making us move forward, and we've been able to make it through together." He added, "Financially, we're not in the same place as we were earlier on in our marriage, but at least we have each other, our son, and we are happy together; that's more important than anything for us.

Andrey & Lisa Wilkins - Long Beach, California
Married 22 Years - Anniversary: September 9, 1989

When Andrey was 20, he started a conversation with Lisa, then 18, that lasted through the holidays, college, service in the Marine Corps, and their move to Southern California. That conversation is still going on after more than 20 years of marriage.

> ## *"Marriage has made me more content with life; it feels good."* —Lisa Wilkins

Andrey was running track at Lisa's college where he noticed her playing volleyball. He attempted to talk to her one day, but didn't get very far. While at home in Spartanburg, South Carolina, for the holidays, he saw her again and decided to take advantage of the opportunity to see if he could make a better attempt at getting to know her.

Their conversations often focused on their mutual interests (they both were athletes), other things they had in common, their families, and thoughts of the lives they wanted to have.

As a result of that second meeting, Andrey and Lisa spent the day together getting to know each other. After three dates, Andrey decided that he was going to marry Lisa.

Since they were enrolled at different colleges, they became pen pals, writing back and forth that fall semester while they were away from each other. That summer, they began dating. They dated for three years, after which they were married while they were still in college.

Finding their way in life and marriage became a little challenging when their schedules took them in opposite directions and made it difficult for them to spend quality time together. Seeing each other in passing without having the luxury of being able to spend the kind of time together they were accustomed to, began to get to each of them. In order to keep the marriage together, they set aside at least one day per week to spend exclusively with each other.

Traveling is one way Andrey and Lisa spend quality time together. The couple has traveled all over the Unted States, Jamacia, Puerto Rico, and Canada. Their first trip to California was a road trip where they stopped in every state along the way to buy souvenirs and take pictures. Once in California, they drove up the coast to San Francisco, then to Lake Tahoe.

"Traveling is different from being at home, because as you travel, you're talking about every little thing and nothing at the same time. Just being in the presence of each other in a different place with different things to see and experience makes all the difference," Andrey says.

The couple agrees that making a conscious effort to communicate also helps to keep their marriage exciting and working, along with showing forgiveness, and most of all, apologizing quickly when necessary.

"Marriage has made me more content with life, and it has given me the knowledge that no matter what happens, I have someone to support me, someone who has my best interest at heart; and for me as a woman, security in a relationship is very important," Lisa says.

Michael B. & Tina Marie Jones - Albuquerque, New Mexico
Married 22 Years - Anniversary: October 14, 1989

Mike's company moved him from San Bernadino, California to Albuquerque, New Mexico. He was visiting California when he went with his cousins to a club in Beverly Hills. Mike liked to dance, so he was working his way around the club making the most of his visit home. As he talked to his cousins, his eyes locked on Tina who was sitting with a few other young ladies at a table not far from them. Mike told his cousins that he was going to marry the young lady he was looking at (Tina). They laughed at him because they knew that he didn't know her.

"We never went to bed without saying to each other, 'I Love You.'" —Tina

A short time later, Mike made his way to their table and asked her to dance. She turned him down. Mike was not the kind to give up, so he waited a bit and asked her again, and she once again turned him down. Mike was determined to meet this young lady, so as she turned him down for at least the third time, he said, "If you change your mind, I'll be nearby talking to my cousins." The next time he asked her to dance, she asked him, "If I dance with you for one song, will you leave me alone?" He agreed, but he knew that if she danced with him just once, he would be in. Sure enough, what was supposed to be "one song" turned into 15.

Mike left the club that night with Tina's phone number and instructions to call the following Thursday. Mike was so excited that he called the following Monday and each day after until he finally talked to her. Tina had given him her work number since he asked for a number where he could reach her. They talked on the work phone for the next month or so until she gave him her home phone number.

This long distance relationship was just beginning to heat up as they became best friends over the phone. It was not long after when Mike asked Tina to visit him in Albuquerque. She did, and for the next three years they both flew back and forth--from New Mexico to California--to see each other. And when they were not with each other, they wrote letters and spent countless hours and dollars on the phone.

After three years, they decided to get married; but before they did, they went through 3 months of counseling with their minister. Once they were married, Tina moved to Albuquerque to be with Mike.

Although Mike and Tina are a bi-racial couple, both speak volumes of their upbringing, which has instilled in them the importance of treating people the way they'd like to be treated, without judging them and having their race get in the way. They say, "We don't look at ourselves as Black and White, we look at ourselves and our kids as Mike and Tina, Jasmine and Ashley. There are no color barriers here in regards to family, friends, neighbors, co-workers or anyone else."

Mike and Tina are settling into a comfortable life together, continually learning and loving each other from day to day. Mike says, "We love our closeness and being together. We try to be as happy as possible without letting little things get us down." Tina points out, "Not only are we married but we like each other, love each other, and we are best friends."

"Mike gets inside your skin and you just can't get him out." —Tina

Wedding vows are taken very seriously in the Jones household. They agreed in the very beginning to never say "I'm leaving you; I want a divorce," or "I want a separation." They committed themselves to remaining together through sickness and health, good times and bad, for richer or poorer.

Chris & Laurie Brown - Long Beach, California

Married 22 Years - Anniversary: November 25, 1989

Chris and Laurie started a friendship as teenagers after meeting at a Sweet 16 party. They dated throughout high school, then they went their separate ways, but remained friends. After Laurie returned home from college, they went out and began to spend more time together. They discovered that they had a lot of things in common. They had a similar mindset: "We saw the world the same way," according to Laurie.

"When I get married, I'm only going to do it one time and I'm going to do it right." —Chris

Chris recalled saying: "When I get married, I'm only going to do it one time with the right person, and I'm going to do it right." This is the same mindset that Laurie shared. The couple agrees that marriage is a partnership, where the couple should be going in the same direction with similar goals while attempting to build their lives together.

Some couples go through sessions of marriage counseling prior to the wedding, administered by their church pastor/minister. Chris and Laurie took things a step further with a no-nonsense approach. They took it upon themselves to sit down together and discuss the marriage and their life together as a married couple, rather than merely focusing on the wedding day—as some couples do. In that discussion, they talked about what they wanted and things they did not want. They discussed things that were not tolerable, in addition to expected behavior, finances, and a whole host of other topics that they considered vital to starting and maintaining a successful union.

In dealing with adversity or concerns within their marriage, Laurie says, "First and foremost, there's God and our faith; we are both obeyers of the Word of God. We've grown together spiritually, and we've learned to cast our cares onto God and not be concerned and worried about things."

Chris and Laurie agree that their marriage is now, and continues to be, successful because of their ability and decision to agree. According to Laurie, "In the Bible, Amos 3:3 says, can two walk together unless they are agreed? Agreement doesn't mean that it's always his way or my way; sometimes it may be his way or my way; sometimes we may meet halfway, a quarter of the way, or three-quarters of the way. But just make up your mind that whatever the issue is, you're going to find a way to agree."

"First and foremost, there's God and our faith..." —Laurie

To help maintain a loving, lasting marriage, Chris and Laurie always put God first. They continue to grow together spiritually, obtaining more knowledge. They continually keep the purpose and vision in the forefront and work towards their common goals.

Andrew & Stacy Thorn - Apple Valley, California
Married 23 Years - Anniversary: August 26, 1988

Andrew and Stacy were attending BYU in Provo, Utah when they were introduced to each other by Stacy's roommate. There were no immediate sparks then, probably because it was the beginning of the school year and they were at a large outdoor party with so many other people around. They saw each other again about four months later at another dance; however, they were both accompanied by their own dates. If they hadn't met at the dance, they would have met eventually, because Andrew's roommate was dating Stacy's friend.

"We've had a great life; we've taken risks and they've paid off." —Andrew

Their dating started out innocent enough. Stacy had planned to travel to Mexico to study and teach for a semester. Andrew helped her with her Spanish since he had already done his missionary work in a Spanish-speaking country. Andrew and Stacy stated that they were not looking to get serious with anyone. They began dating each other 3 or 4 weeks before Stacy was to leave for Mexico, but after about 2 weeks of dating and spending just about every day together, she asked Andrew a question. Her question was: "What do you want from me, Andrew?" Andrew knew this was not a question to be taken lightly, but he didn't have an answer, so he asked her the same question. Stacy said, "I want a blond curly-headed little boy named Cory." Andrew understood that this was her plan for her family in the future. He took that opportunity to answer her by saying, "I want a wife that will love me and support me." Just before Stacy left for Mexico, they had a brief conversation about marriage.

Stacy left for Mexico as scheduled and was away for two and a half months. She returned in June. While she was away, Andrew bought a wedding ring and when she returned, he asked her to marry him. They were engaged in June and were married two months later in August. They had known each other only about three months before they wed. Andrew was 22 years old, and Stacy was 20.

Andrew says, "It was a great time when we first got married; we were together six months before we started having kids. We made it a point to always have time for each other." Andrew and Stacy now have 7 children; Stacy is a stay-at-home mom. "Stacy has given up her career to raise our family, so I work hard so we can support a large family on one income that we've made together." Laughing, Andrew said, "I make all the money and Stacy spends it. I try not to get upset when she spends too much and she tries not to get upset when I don't make enough."

Andrew says initially he was attracted to Stacy's physical beauty along with a magnetic force that she possessed. He says it's hard to explain, but it had a lot to do with the way she treated him. "Stacy asked good questions that seemed to commit me," recalls Andrew. Because of these things, he knew that Stacy was the person he wanted to spend the remainder of his life with.

"Andrew made me feel like I wanted to be better and do better," adds Stacy. "When I was around him, he made me feel like I wanted to be a better person; he motivated me to be a good person."

Andrew and Stacy went into marriage thinking that there was no such thing as divorce. It was not an option for them. Stacy said, "My philosophy has always been that if you think that divorce is a way out, you're not with the right person to make a commitment."

Andrew proudly states, "The greatest blessing in being married to Stacy is that she's always supported me and seen potential in me. She's always seen me to be greater than I am, so I've been able to go out and do things that I know I would not have been able to do if I hadn't had that kind of support. I look at her as if she's going to drive me to a different level.

"We are a partnership that endures time and eternity. We believe that our marriage goes on beyond this life. We are a Team!"

"Our faith has been the anchor in our marriage." —Stacy

Weldon & Tonya Spurling - Long Beach, California
Married 24 Years - Anniversary: May 2, 1987

Tonya had been catching the bus to work in Torrance, California for about eight months. When she left home in the mornings, it was still dark. One particular morning, Weldon waited at the same bus stop, because he was also working in Torrance. When Tonya got to the bus stop, Weldon greeted her with, "Good morning, how are you?" Tonya returned the greeting, but she kept walking to another bus stop. Tonya didn't know Weldon and was a little leery, but she remembered that his greeting to her that morning was nice and polite.

They were on the same bus heading in the same direction. The following days Weldon greeted Tonya and they exchanged small talk. One day while on the bus, Weldon noticed Tonya reading a book titled, *Pure Marital Love*. That was the spark that began their very first conversation about marriage. Weldon's comment referring to marriage was, "It doesn't work." Tonya replied, "God created it to work." Tonya suggested to Weldon that he read the book, and afterwards they could continue their conversation. Weldon actually read the book, and to his surprise--for the first time--he had a better understanding of marriage. Weldon had been married for about 6 years, but it ended in divorce.

Tonya says marriage for her was a spiritual journey, because she asked God to send her a mate. "Before meeting Weldon, I prayed and asked God for a husband. I was specific with what I wanted and needed in a husband, and I trusted that God would bring the right person to me."

"We gave our marriage to God in the beginning and said, 'Do what You need to do to keep us together.'" —Weldon

Weldon and Tonya went on a date to a concert, and on the way back from the concert, Tonya was noticeably restless. She finally said to Weldon, "I'm celibate." Her comment didn't seem to phase Weldon, even though his intention from the beginning was, as he said, to "hit that." Weldon says, "It didn't matter; there was something special about her."

Both Weldon and Tonya stopped taking the bus to work, and as a result, lost contact for a few months until they saw each other at a McDonald's near Tonya's house. They sat and talked that day and have been together ever since. After about six months together, Tonya realized Weldon was the person she was going to spend the remainder of her life with.

"After we got back together, I accepted Christ as my Savior in her kitchen," recalls Weldon. "I had visions where I'd see her in the kitchen cooking, and me sitting on the couch; and I'd see her as my wife--and it was a very pleasing feeling."

"Marriage means that I did something godly right, and it is still right, because I see it every day." —Tonya

14 months from the day they met, Weldon and Tonya were married. Weldon says their honeymoon night was one of the most memorable moments in their 23 years of marriage, because he was celibate also. Laughing at the memory, Weldon commented, "I can still smell the sulfur from the fireworks going off, today!"

According to Tonya, their marriage is successful because they always talk, always…in any and all circumstances. "There is never a day that goes by that we don't have conversations. Not just talking for a few minutes, (but) real conversations. We have always been first for each other."

According to Weldon, "When we got married, we made the agreement that Tonya would stay at home and raise the family, I would work and I would work as hard as I needed to work to keep them in the lifestyle they deserved. Sometimes that meant working 24 hours, but whatever I brought home was as much hers as mine."

Darryl & Tammy Towns - Perris, California
Married 25 Years - Anniversary: March 29. 1986

Darryl and Tammy Towns are perfect examples of what happens when you dial a wrong number that turns out to be the right number. Twenty four years ago, Tammy was calling a friend, but mistakenly dialed Darryl's house. Darryl answered the phone and spoke with Tammy. She thought she was actually speaking to her friend, believing Darryl was her friend, pretending he wasn't. When she called again, however, it wasn't a wrong number, she called deliberately to speak to Darryl. They talked on the phone for awhile before they decided to go out on a date. Although they had never met, they knew a lot of the same people. Darryl figured that if she knew some of the same people he went to high school with, she was good people. Darryl learned that Tammy often attended church; this knowledge was important, because he was raised in the church and wanted his girlfriend and future wife to be involved in the church also.

"After all these years, I'm still in love with Darryl." —Tammy

As they dated, they wanted to go through all the seasons together so that they would get to know each other in as many different situations as they could. They dated about four years before they decided they wanted to be married. Darryl says after about a year, he knew that Tammy was the one he wanted to spend the remainder of his life with. Tammy was 21 years old when they were married and Darryl was 24. Growing up, both Tammy and Darryl had witnessed, firsthand, the inner workings of a healthy, loving marriage through the examples set by their parents.

Because of their distinctly different personalities, Tammy and Darryl are not always on the same page when it comes to making decisions, and that sometimes creates tension. Darryl says, "We still fight, but above all, we still love each other. It helps us because we get everything out in the open and we are then able to move on. It helps us to keep loving each other, and that helps to keep our marriage successful."

"You have to keep working to make your marriage successful, everyday," explains Darryl as he tells how he and Tammy date each other as if they are still boyfriend and girlfriend. They may call each other at work and set up a date for a movie, dinner, or drinks. He believes this keeps their marriage exciting and spontaneous.

Darryl and Tammy acknowledge that their marriage has been the grounding force that has helped them focus on and accomplish all the goals they've set for their lives thus far. They both agree that faith in God and their love for each other has kept them together all these years, along with the fact that they put each other first--which causes every aspect of their marriage to continually get better.

"When you are in love with your spouse, you can't get her off your mind." —Darryl

Janet was volunteering at a Catholic Church bingo fundraiser when she saw Pete. No one was with him. She thought maybe he was waiting for his wife, but later, as she came back around, he was still there alone. She was thinking, "He doesn't play as if he's played very much." The game was being played for money, so it was played a little differently than regular bingo. Janet went over to his table to help him with the game. She stayed with him for the duration of the game, which he won. As Pete was leaving, he asked Janet if he could take her home, but she politely said she had a way home. Pete says, "I knew she was lying, but I let it go."

Pete came again to play bingo, and when Janet saw him, she smiled. Pete thought, "She's glad to see me!" After bingo, Janet allowed Pete to take her out to eat and have drinks. Pete said, "I took her home, walked her to the door, kissed her on the forehead, told her I had a great time, and went home." He smiles, and says, "I blew her mind; she didn't know what to think, 'cause she thought I was going to make a move on her. I knew what I was doing, so I said I was going to play it just right." Pete thinks back and says, "I played her 'til she got me!"

"I've learned to be more considerate, it's not just me any more." —Pete

That night was the beginning of their relationship. (Pete had gotten married the first time when he was just 16 years old. He says it was a very painful marriage and breakup, and he hadn't planned on marrying again.) Janet was 34 years old, had never been married, and had no plans of ever getting married. She was going to be a career woman. Janet's parents were married for only a couple of years, as a result, she was raised by her grandparents. Her grandfather died when she was 5, so she had never lived in a house with a father of any kind.

Although before meeting Janet, Pete had no plans of marrying again, he proposed to Janet 2 months after they met. Pete confesses that not only did he feel comfortable with Janet, but he also believed he could really trust her. "I love her honesty and compassion. She was different from the other women I had dated." Janet says, "Pete was a lot of fun, and I really enjoyed him. He had become my best friend. We had great times." Janet accepted Pete's proposal but said she would not be available for marriage until the following year, because she had things she had to get in order before she was married.

"Marriage means being able to share your life with someone that you truly love, no matter what." —Janet

The wedding was set for June 25, 1983. Wedding invitations were sent out and relatives were coming in from out of town. As fate would have it, however, when Pete and Janet were married, Pete was confined to a wheel chair. He was driving drunk and had a stroke, which resulted in a head-on collision with a city bus. The wedding date could not be changed so they went ahead with the wedding. Janet says, "I had to really love him to go through with the marriage and stay, because Pete was in a wheel chair for the first year of our marriage."

Pete finally became miserable enough to admit he had a drinking problem and went through recovery. He explained, "I didn't want either myself or Janet to have to go through the kind of pain I caused ever again." Janet remembers that prior to his recovery, "Pete was not the man I actually married, but I knew there was good in him. He had goals and dreams for our lives, so I was committed to help him get through those bad times." Janet joined the group Al-Anon so that she could assist herself in helping him deal with his problems and get through them victoriously.

"Our marriage is successful because of our ability to communicate," says Janet. "The things we don't like, we share with each other, as well as the things we do like. We stay excited about seeing each other. We don't live separate lives; our lives are strictly a unit--after all, we are best friends."

Janet says, laughing, "I married him for his money, so I was going to stay with him until he makes it."

Note: Pete Bryant passed January 26, 2009, before photography was done for this book.

Pete & Janet Bryant - Carson, California
Married 26 Years - Anniversary: June 25, 1983

Floyd met Carla while she was out celebrating her 22nd birthday in Atlanta, Georgia. Carla was attending the University of Georgia in Athens. They got to know each other by spending time talking on the phone and seeing each other when she came home for the holidays.

Both Floyd and Carla were asking the same questions about mates, family, and spiritual matters at the same time. Carla went so far as to write what she wanted in a husband. "I wanted a husband that was a Christian, someone that would be a good father and husband. Floyd explains, "I was searching spiritually. I can remember asking God to bring me someone for me, I can't pick them, I give up; I just wanted to know what God wanted me to do with the remainder of my life."

Their backgrounds, philosophies, values, and goals were similar. In addition, they agreed on a lot of things as they grew closer with each passing day. It didn't take long for Floyd and Carla to realize that they wanted to be with each other in holy matrimony. So, approximately six months after they met, they were engaged; a year later, they were married with intentions of spending the remainder of their lives together.

"A husband and wife have to continue to grow together." —Floyd

On October 5, 1985—more than 26 years ago—Floyd and Carla were married at West End Church of God in Christ in Atlanta, Georgia. There was a small number of guests in attendance; Floyd's brother was best man and Carla's sister was maid of honor. They didn't have a huge wedding because they didn't have a lot of money; besides, they were more interested in their life after the wedding, and getting things off to a great start.

Just before Floyd proposed to Carla, he purchased a new car. After his decision to marry Carla, he took his new car back to the dealership.

His reasoning was if he was going to get married, he could not afford to have a new car payment at the same time.

Their wedding display spoke volumes about the style in which they would conduct their life together. This would be a marriage of two people who had so much in common. Neither of them are materialistic in their style of living. Their family lives were very similar; they both came from the homes of hard working, middle class parents. Both their parents were married at a young age and both families were going through a divorce while Floyd and Carla were in college. Their parents' divorces were obviously not a deterent. In fact, it brought them even closer together because they were on common ground, and they talked in-depth about their parents' divorces and its implications for them in their marriage.

"I wanted a husband that was a Christian, someone that would be a good father and husband." —Carla

As with many marriages, the road is not always paved, and there are rough spots along the way. Floyd and Carla had their financial struggles early on in their marriage, but since they were not materialistic people and had similar goals, they were able to work together to get through those rough times.

Floyd and Carla credit their church and church family for helping to add stability to their marriage by setting and being great examples of Christian behavior. According to Floyd, "By having a spiritual anchor, we've been blessed together as husband and wife to be able to overcome challenges that may have otherwise knocked us out of the game."

Friendship, communication, mutual respect for each other, and their belief in God are the cornerstones of their relationship.

Floyd & Carla Williams - Atlanta, Georgia
Married 26 Years - Anniversary: October 5, 1985

Edward and Laura worked the night shift together as nurses in the ICU at a hospital in Montebello when they were in their early twenties. They didn't talk much until they started going out after work with a group of other nurses and employees from the hospital. They enjoyed the times they were together with their co-workers, and eventually began spending more time together, just the two of them.

According to Ed, "We started doing things separately from the group, and we enjoyed those times. As we got to knew each other better, we fell in love with each other." Laura says, "I was attracted to him. I thought he was nice and kind. After a while, I began to think we could build a future together. Ed was not a big drinker or gambler, and I thought he'd make a good father for the children I thought we'd have."

Ed and Laura knew each other about 6 months prior to their engagement; they were engaged a year before marrying. After the wedding, Ed and Laura went about the business of creating a life and family together.

"We've been able to endure."—Laura

Like most married couples, their union was not without stressful times. Because they were aware of how money matters can play a big role in the success or failure of one's marriage, Ed and Laura wanted to be as wise as possible in that area. As a result, the couple sought financial advice so that they could begin their union on the right track. Ed remembers living through tough financial times with his parents, so he wanted to do things differently in his marriage. Despite having had financial advice early on, they still encountered some difficult money issues. During those times, they'd reevaluate the situation, whatever that situation might be, and then they would come up with a new plan to deal with it.

Laura explains, "Our marriage has gone through different stages. We've gone through the financial stage; now, and for the past five years, Ed has gone through some challenges with his job. And we've had to deal with the situation, because when the job comes home, it's not always easy; it puts pressure on the relationship and the happiness at home." To help make things better at home, Ed started taking better care of himself. He changed his diet, started eating better, began doing his exercises, and that helped him to more effectively handle the stress of situations at home and at work.

"We didn't fall apart or break up; we're still together and still love each other." —Ed

There was a time in the 27 years Ed and Laura have been married that they lost touch with each other. They were living side-by-side, but not engaged in the relationship the way they once were. To help them get to the next stage in their marriage, they went for marriage counseling. Ed said, "Counseling has helped to keep things moving forward."

According to Laura, "Our marriage is successful because I was non-confrontational. I took a lot, because I wanted us to make our marriage work. I was always asking, 'How can we make our marriage better?'" Ed added, "I came to a place where I was grateful and thankful for Laura. We went through some difficult times, but each time, we came through it. The bottom line is, I didn't want to be divorced; she didn't either, because we loved each other. We knew we were going through changes, and we had to adjust to them—and we still are; it's always an adjustment. Our love is strong, it's enduring, we're committed, and because of that, we are still together!"

Edward & Laura Jimenez - Pomona, California
Married 27 Years - Anniversary: April 28, 1984

Alex & Angela Rambo - Long Beach, California
Married 27 Years - Anniversary: Sept. 1, 1984

The first time Alex and Angela met was at a choir concert at New Hope Baptist Church in Long Beach, California. They both were there to see their friends perform. They sat on the same row with a very talkative little boy between them. The little boy asked each of them their names and introduced them to each other. At the time they met, Alex was a senior in high school and Angela was a junior.

"I worked on myself to become better for her." *—Alex*

After graduation, Alex and Angela attended Long Beach City College. Alex would see Angela with some of his friends, and they would run into each other in groups as they socialized around campus.

As time passed, Angela was driving her newly purchased car around the neighborhood when she saw Alex and a friend playing basketball in front of his house. After driving around the block a few times, she stopped and talked to Alex one-on-one. It was then that she realized that there was a natural attraction between the two of them. Although they both had dates later that evening, they cancelled them so that they could spend more time with each other. "After about three or four months of dating, I told her I was going to marry her," Alex recalls. "I was so overwhelmed by her character, personality, and integrity--everything about her was so good."

In the meantime, life happened. Alex went to school in Oregon for awhile, and Angela continued attending college in Long Beach. The attraction he felt for Angela was so strong that he came back to Long Beach to be near her so that she could be a part of his college life and the successes he was experiencing.

Approximately 5 years later, and with a 10-month old daughter, Alex and Angela were married. They were married in 1984, but by the late 80s, though the country was not necessarily in a recession, people were hurting for jobs. This included Alex. Alex lost his job and was unemployed for almost a year. Finances were tight, and became a major source of stress between them; they found themselves communicating at each other as opposed to with each other. Angela was working full time, but that was not quite enough without Alex's income; as a result, they had to declare bankruptcy.

The Rambo's marriage at that time was not as happy as it once was, the stress level was high, the funds were low, and to make matters worse, they were not communicating. Divorce was not an option, so they decided that they needed the help of a third party, and they made an appointment for marriage counseling. They went to the first session, but were unable to go back, because they could not afford the cost of counseling.

"If I die tomorrow, because I'm married to Angela, I'll die the happiest man on the face of the earth." —Alex

Alex explains, "Sometimes in a relationship, you have to take a step back (one of us), and look at the big picture. The big picture is: Do you want to be here? And you answer to yourself correctly—this is not an option or choice thing—'Yes,' you want to be here. You don't have a choice, so what do you do to make things work? That's when I had to learn to take myself out of the equation to find out what she needed to be comfortble and less stressed and, at the same time, it alleviated my stress because she was happier. Once she's happy, everything is cool."

The turning point in their marriage came late one night as they sat on the floor after arguing and trying to work through things. That's when Alex apologized. He apologized for putting them through the things they were going through. He acknowledged that his being out of work for so long was the cause of stress in their marriage. That acknowledgment was a major step toward them working things out both financially and with communication between themselves.

Gene & Damita Johnson - Carson, California

Married 27 Years - Anniversary: October 22, 1984

Gene Johnson saw Damita at a video arcade in Marina Del Rey, California. That first look was enough to make Gene go over and introduce himself. They went out the same night, and while on their first date, Gene told Damita everything about himself: the good, the bad, and the ugly. When he finished, she was still there. Gene says, "From the very first day I met her, I knew she was the one."

Three months later, they were living together. A few months after they had been living together, Damita asked Gene what his intentions were regarding her. His reply was that he was going to marry her when things were right. Things got right pretty quickly, because they became engaged *that* day. Approximately six months after they met, Gene and Damita were married.

Neither of them had any great expectations of their marriage since both their previous marriages had ended in divorce. Damita had been married for 6 six months, and Gene had been married 2 years. There had not been a stable, long standing marriage in either of their families, so they had no role models when it came to marriage.

"When the two of you become one and you are at odds with each other, you are just fighting against yourself." —Damita

Gene and Damita's marriage went through some very hard times. They were care free, taking risks, getting involved with the wrong people, doing the wrong things and generally making a mess of things. They were living beyond their means, and the financial pressures along with everything else, created tension in the relationship.

Their lives didn't improve until they both made the decision to give their lives to the Lord. Damita says, "If we had not gotten saved, we probably would not be married. That's the honest truth. It was when we gave our lives to God that things really started to change. God makes a successful marriage." Gene added, "God and work; you got to work at it. Anything that's worth having requires work. God gave us something to work on."

"Marriage without God is like shooting dice; it's a crap shoot." —Gene

Maturity and following God's principles helped them to implement better financial disciplines. Instead of using credit cards, they used a debit card. Gene says, "With a debit card, you can't spend what you don't have." After they made the decision to live by God's principles, divorce was not an option, so a lot of the things they were fighting about didn't make any sense any more. Damita points out, "When the two of you become one, and you're at odds with each other, you're just fighting against yourself."

Gene said, "The first 2 years of our marriage were rocky. It was challenging because I'm always right and so is she. That was a problem back then, so I took her to the Lord and I said, 'Okay Lord, now what's up? This woman's got a problem,' and the Lord said, 'I agree 100%--and the problem is *you*!' The Lord began to tell me and show me how to have the woman of my dreams, but it required work, not me changing her, but *me changing myself*. Marriage without God is like shooting dice; it's a crap shoot."

Gene continued, "My wife is my best friend. She has paid the price. To put up with me for 27 years, she deserves a medal, because I don't even think I could do it. You can't be together for 27 years and expect for things to always stay the same, because people are constantly changing. I understand that God is her first love, and she understands that God is my first love, and our relationship together is based on each of our relationships with Him."

Gavin & Marquita Curry - Los Angeles, California
Married 27 years - Anniversary: October 23, 1984

It was the summer of 1976, a summer full of fond memories for Gavin and Marquita. The summer of '76 is when they met. Gavin was hanging out with his cousin, in of all places, summer school--especially odd since he was not enrolled there.

Marquita couldn't help but notice Gavin, because after seeing him come to school in shorts she said, "He has nice legs!" Those nice legs left enough of an impression on her to pretend her books were too heavy to carry so that Gavin would carry them for her. It worked, because Gavin not only carried her books, but he carried them all the way home, even though he lived on the other side of the city.

That was just the beginning. They soon developed a very close friendship, staying up late at night talking on the phone. Marquita introduced Gavin to her grandfather, and because Gavin was very mannerable, her grand-dad liked him right away. They dated off and on for the next few years.

During their senior year in high school, Marquita bought a dress in preparation for the prom, but she didn't have a date. Gavin did the gentlemanly thing and took her to the prom and to grad night afterwards.

"I was attached to our friendship."
—Marquita

Their friendship continued as Gavin left for college. When he returned from college in 1981, he and Marquita began dating once again. They dated until 1982 when they became engaged. Marquita said to Gavin, "Either we're going to get married or break up." They were married in October of 1984.

Gavin and Marquita's marriage has remained in tact over the years because of their friendship, their love for each other, and their faith in God, they also had a desire and willingness to have a successful marriage for the well being of their family, both immediate and extended.

This couple's willingness to have a successful marriage does not mean they have not experienced difficulties. Over the past 26 years, they've only spent one night apart out of anger. Gavin says, "If I leave the room, she'll follow, because she's a talker." She likes to talk through the problem(s) or misunderstanding(s) they're having. Gavin says, "Having a king-sized bed doesn't hurt either." When the situations arise, they are not against having outside help in the form of counseling; over the years they've been to counseling a few times, and it has worked very well for them.

"There is nothing separate about my life; it's shared; it's our life."
—Gavin

Dealing with finances could be a deal breaker for new couples and sometimes couples who have been together for years. Marquita says, "We've had some horrible, heated arguments over money." Gavin and Marquita got married in their early 20's, so they had a lot to learn in regards to handling money as a couple. Gavin said, "The first time I was in a bank was with Marquita. I didn't know anything about savings and things like that." Although Gavin and Marquita say their finances are still a struggle, early on, they were able to get on the same page where money was concerned and set up controls for retirement and other such necessities. They say they manage, but they'd like to do a lot better.

Gavin and Marquita agree that if all else failed, they'd be able to carry on because of the friendship they've built over the years. They say their marriage continues to be a work in progress, particularly because they are so wrapped up in their children's lives, they forget to make time for themselves.

"Marriage means a life long commitment. I'm in it for the long haul, and I look forward to us growing old together. Being married helps develop that part of you that is not about you, it's the *collective* you," explains Marquita.

Edward & Grace Resendez - Pomona, California
Married 31 Years - Anniversary: Anniversary: April 12, 1980

Edward Resendez and his friends were shooting pool in the back house at his girlfriend's house when another friend stopped by with Grace. They were on their way to a double date. Edward recalls that when Grace walked in, it was as if the music stopped and all eyes were on her. He remembers she was very attractive and wore a micro mini dress.

He was introduced to Grace, and for a moment their eyes locked. After leaving, Grace says, "I was walking out and I just knew that Ed would play a very important part in my life. I knew I would see him again." That was the very beginning of their relationship even though Edward had a girlfriend, and Grace had a boyfriend at the time. Following that first meeting, the two of them didn't see each other again for a few months.

"What a journey!! It's been quite a journey!" —Ed

They saw each other at a party given by the the same friend who Grace was with when she first met Ed. This time, however, neither of them were dating anyone. Grace came to the party with her mom and 9 month old son. They danced together and talked. After the party, Ed took Grace and her son home. (Her mom had already left.) The following day, he went to a family gathering with Grace, and after that, they continued to date.

Grace says, "It was easy to date Ed, because from the very beginning, he treated my son, Michael, as if he was his own son. He was creating a special bond with him. They took her son on their dates with them. They went to places on their dates where kids were welcomed because they wanted him with them.

Ed and Grace had been spending all their spare time together. Ed was a senior in college when they decided to move in together. They lived together for two years. During the years they dated, they broke up a

few times, citing things being a little different when you live together as opposed to just dating.

Grace became pregnant in 1980 with Edward's child. Having had one child out of wedlock, Grace decided that she would have the baby only if they were married before it was born. Edward wanted Grace to have his child, so he acknowledged his love for her and asked her to marry him. The wedding was planned in a week, and the couple was married the following week in her mother's back yard.

There were some dark times in their marriage. Grace says, "The first 12 years of marriage was not good, because Ed drank and stayed out late, leaving me home with the kids." She admits that "This was the source of a great deal of resentment." Grace says she thought of leaving many times but she liked the fact that being able to be a stay at home Mom allowed her to have complete involvement in the nuturing of her children.

Through counseling, compromise, God, church, prayer, and Ed deciding that he wanted to keep his family together, they were able to build a successful marriage.

Over these 31 years, they've been able to work through their issues by having God in their lives and being able to compromise. Now, they've grown and matured together and are able to communicate with each other, rather than not talking for days on end.

"Marriage has given me love and a great family." —Ed

Grace explained that their marriage is sucessful because God has been a big part of their lives since the beginning. "We would not be together if it were not for God, Church, and prayer." Grace exclaims with a smile, "It took a lot to get here! I love change!"

Randal & Cindy Linde - Lakewood, California

Married 31 Years - Anniversary: November 3, 1979

Randal Linde had been divorced four years before he met Cindy. He wasn't dating very much because his divorce left him with full custody of his two daughters, ages one and three. Randal thought about marrying again, but he wasn't sure it would actually happen because his main concern was raising his two daughters. Cindy had thoughts of marriage, too, but she knew that she didn't want a repeat of her parents' marriage. Her parents divorced when she was 15.

"I told her, 'Everything I've promised you will come true'—it just took 30 years to happen!" —Randal

Randal and Cindy met on the job when she was introduced to all the full time employees on her first day of work. She was a temporary employee working in the same area with Randal. While talking to Cindy, he found out she was single, had never been married, and didn't have a family. "I liked what I saw, liked what I heard, and I asked her to go out with me."

Cindy almost canceled their first date because she was a little nervous. She thought Randal was a little too worldly since he had already been married, divorced, and was raising two kids; yet, he was only 26 years old.

Their first date was great, and as a result, Cindy knew that Randal was the man she wanted to spend the remainder of her life with. She says because of Randal's size, he's always made her feel safe in his arms. He was also the first man to declare his love for her.

Recalling his proposal, Randal says, "I asked Cindy if she was through playing and having a good time. If you are, we can do a good thing here." According to Cindy, "When I met someone and got married, I knew the direction I wanted to go as a family, and Randal wanted to go in the very same direction. It was really easy to talk and communicate our desires for our family. We wanted the same things, and most importantly, we wanted each other.

Approximately six months after his proposal, Randal and Cindy were married.

Cindy says that her thoughts about marriage were, "You land the guy, you get married and everything is just glorious; however, marriage has taught me a lot about patience. You have to work on things all the time, and it taught me that you don't just snap your fingers, things happen, and you live happily ever after. There is so much compromise involved."

One of their major challenges during their marriage had been Randal's 5-year cycles with employment. Things would go great for 5 years, then the following 5 years would be a financial disaster. Cindy says, "Money is probably always a challenge for any couple; we became very creative on what to do when we didn't have any. We never gave up; we just kept thinking how can we pull ourselves up? What can we do to make our finances better?" Things started looking better after Randal and Cindy got rid of their credit cards, paid their bills, and started to control their spending by using cash. Randal went back to school and trained in the medical field. They were then able to see their dream of owning a home come true. Randal said, "I told her, 'Everything I've promised you, will come true'—it just took 30 years to happen!"

"Money is probably a challenge for any new couple..." —Cindy

Randal and Cindy explain that their marriage is successful because, "We're a great blalance for each other. What I lack, he has, and vice versa. We've learned to meet in the middle. Our morals are the same, and we have a strong belief in God as He guides us each day. We also make time for each other. It could be moments or days. We spend at least one day each week together. We thought we were in love to no ends of the earth 31 years ago when we were married, but it's just *sooo* much more than that 31 years later!" she beams.

Willie & Cynthia Anderson - Decatur, Georgia

Married 31 Years - Anniversary: August 11, 1979

While home on leave from military service, Will was looking through a local high school year book when he came across Cynthia's photo. There was something about her photo that made him want to get to know her. He later learned that his cousin was the best friend to Cynthia's sister. He was able to get Cynthia's phone number through his cousin. They communicated by phone after he returned to his post of service at Fort Benning in south Georgia. Cynthia was a student at the University of Georgia. Will was able to go to Athens on the weekends to visit Cynthia, and while he was away, they spent a lot of time talking on the phone.

By the time Will's enlistment in the military came to an end, Cynthia had transferred from the University to the now defunct Atlanta College of Art in Atlanta. Will remembers visiting Cynthia in Atlanta when she was a resident manager in the dorm there. Will says, "I was there past curfew when the fire alarm sounded. I didn't come out because everyone would see me in her apartment after hours, so as Cynthia left me to check on the alarm, she said to me, 'I'll call you if it's a real fire!'" Will said it was then that he knew Cynthia had accepted him as the person she wanted to spend the remainder of her life with. Since he was willing to stay in a building that was possibly on fire to protect her, he knew they had gotten past the questioning stage of their relationship.

Will was discharged from the military in May of 1979, and he moved to Atlanta to get a job and be with Cynthia. They were married in August of the same year, three years after they met.

"Living with my wife is a work in progress from day to day, and I love her more and more for each of those days!" —Will

Will and Cynthia credit their faith in God and their assurance that they will continuously be there for each other as the foundation of their long marriage. Cynthia also said, "We are successful in our marriage because we are tolerant of each other, and we realize that neither of us is always right all the time."

"Our marriage continues to stay strong because we've been able to work out our differences." —Will

"Our marriage continues to stay strong because we've been able to work out our differences. We each know the other's personality, what the other will and will not do, and knowing those things makes it easier for us to accept each other for who we are without either of us attempting to change the other. My wife and I are so different, but you don't get to pick who you fall in love with," says Will.

Will also said, "I love Cynthia for her neatness. I've not been in a house as clean as she keeps our house. It used to drive me crazy! I couldn't put down a glass and expect to use it again because she'd come behind me, wash it and put it away. If I don't put my keys on the key hook, I might not be able to find them because she'll move them. I've learned to live with it." Cynthia replies with a laugh, "I realize that I have not been able to change Willie's messiness, but I keep working on him!"

Ali'i & Aurora Ho'malu - Redding, California

Married 32 years - Anniversary: August 25, 1979

Aurora lived with her family on the military base on the west side of the island of Oahu, Hawaii, where her father was a Naval officer. One day Aurora and a friend were walking through their neighborhood selling homemade chocolate chip cookies door-to-door, raising money for a youth camp, when she knocked on a door and got no answer—but heard a voice coming from a nearby car. As she walked past the car, Ali'i stuck his head from beneath the hood of the car, where he was in the process of rebuilding the engine. Aurora's friend knew Ali'i from their canoeing club. As the two of them began to talk, she introduced the young man to Aurora. During the conversation, whenever the opportunity presented itself, Aurora would plug the cookies in an effort to make a sale.

Ali'i was 19 then, and Aurora was 16. She and her friend left without a sale, but later, Ali'i asked his friend for Aurora's phone number. He called a few days later and they began having regular phone conversations. Since they both were active in their respective churches, they had a common ground from which to start communications. In the beginning, Aurora made it clear to Ali'i that she didn't want anything but a friendship; she was devoted to her family, her church life, and other responsibilities. In essence, she was very busy and committed to doing things that mattered to her and her family.

"If we can perceive each other as a gift, a lot of the ridiculous expectations will fall away." —Aurora

Ali'i says, "When I first met her, I knew in my heart that she was the one. There was a grace about her. I liked the way she carried herself; there was a certain level of discipline and confidence about her.
It took Aurora about a year to realize that Ali'i wanted to build a relationship that would lead to marriage. Aurora explains, "I had to do a lot of praying, because I knew marriage was a covenant and could not be broken; it had to be forever. I had to be willing to ride the wave and surf the waters while putting my entire being into marriage."
In premarital counseling, Ali'i and Aurora went through the "Love Walk," the foundation for planting seeds of God's love for each other in their

hearts so that no matter what occurred, their marriage would survive. Ali'i and Aurora had their wedding at the Oahu Botanical Gardens along a pathway lined with plumaria flowers. Aurora remembers, "During our marriage, intense adjustments were required for us because our backgrounds were extremely different. We had different world views. It wasn't that I was not Hawaiian, I was fair-skinned, which was not a big plus on the island. It was an issue with the culture, community, and some family members; on top of that, I was a military dependent, so if you are fair-skinned and a military dependent, that created a double whammy.

"When I first met her, I knew in my heart that she was the one." —Ali'i

"Those adjustments created some challenging situations for my family; it was really great, though. I would not exchange that experience for anything. It was probably the most profound and positive experience that I've ever had, and I'm grateful. I was able to see what it was like to be on the lowest end of the totem pole, because I was not wanted or accepted. I experienced a lot of prejudice and discrimination. I had to have an escort to get around school, and my family received death threats. The ethnic tension was very intense during those times. There was a lot of marital tension between us since our backgrounds and scheme of thought were so different. During those times, we just held on to what was common beween us, which was Jesus Christ and our love for Him."

According to Ali'i, "Sometimes you have to go through a lot of turmoil to find your way, and common ground. The first ten years were pretty tough, but once we passed the ten-year mark, things started to smooth out." Ali'i says, "From my perspective, in our marriage for 32 years, our common ground has been the Lord. That's been our glue, our bridge, our life raft in the most troubling and heartbreaking times."

Aurora says, "Our marriage for me has been like this life-saver in the middle of this huge unknown environment that surrounds us, and I know that everything will be ok; we'll be perfectly safe while staying afloat."

James Lobdell & Vickie Kropenske - Inglewood - California
Married 33 Years - Anniversary: January 28, 1978

James and Vickie met in New York where James was attending Seminary, studying to be a pastor. Vickie had already attained a degree in Sociology, but she was in New York attending Hunter College studying nursing. She worked as a switchboard operator in James' dorm. In order to get phone messages, he had to see Vickie. When James went to get his messages, she was abrupt with him, so there was no connection in the beginning. Vickie says James walked around with a pocket protector and his books, so she thought "he was a nerd."

"If you make your own life interesting, you make the relationship interesting." —Vickie

Both James and Vickie had graduated by the time they began dating, as they both continued to live and work in New York. They would go to what James called, "A wonderful place that served lots of different kinds of pies. Vickie and I would go there and have pie and coffee and talk. It was talking and sharing at first, not dating."

James recalls, "We'd share feelings and ideas, and we felt a connection that way. We were not feeling a romantic connection, but we were able to share our deepest thoughts and ideas. I could share with her, and she'd hear without being judgmental, and that meant a lot to me." James added that, "We were both in caring professions, and we'd share our work with each other. We had similar values in terms of what we believed was important in life."

As they continued to share, their relationship evolved, and approximately 4 years after they met, they decided to marry. Their commitment to each other and their marriage was put to the test early. They had been married a little over a year when James was asked to pastor a church thousands of miles away in Inglewood, California. That position meant that he and Vickie would have to give up their jobs, friends, and everything else they had been establishing since college to move across country to a place where they knew no one. They were entering a new situation, and had no idea what they would face once they got there. James says of Vickie,

"She had faith and trust, along with the fact that she was willing to make that step feeling that it would all work out."

Things did work out, but not right away. Once in California, things did not go according to plan, but they worked together to make the best of the situation. To make matters even more difficult, within 6 to 9 months after arriving in Inglewood, Vickie's mom became critically ill and passed away; James developed a ruptured appendix which almost took his life, and his mother passed; they had two cars stolen, then the rental car they had was also stolen! Vickie says, "Coming through all that in such a short amount of time, we felt if we could manage all that, we could manage anything!"

Both James and Vickie lead very busy lives: James is Pastor of Holy Trinity Lutheran Church in Inglewood, and Vickie is a visiting nurse, among a whole host of her other duties, including being a pastor's wife. With two very busy people, there are instances where seemingly there isn't enough time for each other. James said, "Making time for each other has been a challenge our whole marriage." In order to make sure they'd spend more time together—just the two of them, they established a date night. On their date night, James and Vickie go out to dinner and leave their cell phones at home. They also take vacations to places where they can do interesting things. They've traveled together to South Africa, Israel, and other fascinating destinations around the world. When they return home, they use the things of interest, which they were involved in while traveling, to help them provide better service to others in ways that make a difference.

"I trust that no matter what, and through it all, we'll be together." —James

Vickie explains, "I'm not sure that 'always and forever' is something that you truly feel. I think that's something that we've developed over time because we share a faith, values, and a sense of commitment. If you share a faith, it helps to give you the framework or road map to set parameters for what the relationship is or becomes."

Max was hanging out with his best friend, Gabriel, when Frances and her sister called to talk to Gabriel's brother. Frances and Max began talking then, and have been talking ever since. Frances and Max talked on the phone for at least a month getting to know each other before they met. When they met, they were in the company of a group of their friends. Max was 17 at the time, and Frances said she was 16. Max learned some time later that she was only 13. Their relationship grew stronger with the passing days and months. After Max graduated from high school, they were married. Max was then 18 and Frances was 14.

"Marriage takes a lot of giving and a lot of understanding." —Frances

Their parents were not very happy with their decision. But eventually, both Max's and Frances' parents came around once they realized they were in love with each other. Now, after years have passed, and Max and Frances have remained married for 33 years, there are no questions of their love for each other and the success of their marriage and family.

Being married for 33 years has not been easy according to Max and Frances. Times were really tough in the beginning. Frances was 15 and had just given birth to their son, and she was thinking of breaking up. Max would not hear of it and was able to convince Frances to stick with him and make it work. They say, "We started from ground zero. It's not easy, especially when you have nothing and are trying to get ahead; it's

also a lot harder when you're younger." Max says, "Now, I think it's best to start out with nothing, that's how you really learn to appreciate things when you get them. It was a struggle, but we loved each other so much we made it work." They admit that it was sometimes very frustrating, but they were dedicated to each other and to the success and longevity of their marriage.

When Max was younger, he had a very difficult time finding gainful employment. Being fresh out of high school with no formal higher education proved difficult in the beginning. "I'm a hard worker and I'll try anything legal to provide for my family." He went from company to company working low wage jobs until he decided that he needed to learn computers. He taught himself to work on computers, then later took courses to learn more.

During those days, they struggled with finances as Frances worked, while Max went to school. "We pulled together and worked through it," says Frances. "Over the years, we've gone full circle, with Max not working while going to school, then I was a stay at home mom, to now, where Max is unemployed and I'm working." Max commented, "We adjust! We have a very unique marriage because we were married so young. We grew together and we've been able to make it work."

"Our marriage is successful," says Frances, "because we have open communication, we are true to each other, we pray every morning and every night, we have lots of understanding, and we are willing, with Gods' help, to stick it out through the bad times and the good times; after all, if you get through the hard times, you can make it through anything!"

"...if you get through the hard times, you can make it through anything!" —Frances

Max & Frances Gallegos - Wilmington, California
Married 33 Years - Anniversary: March 20, 1978

Rigoberto & Maria Leticia Marquez - South Gate, California

Married 33 Years - Anniversary: October 6, 1978

Rigoberto and Maria grew up in Mexico. Rigoberto came to the United States when he was 20 and Maria came when she was 16 years old. Some years later, they met one evening at a club in Los Angeles.

Rigoberto saw Maria sitting with an "old lady" and decided to ask her to dance. Two other men had the same idea; the three of them came to the table at once. Maria looked at the three men who asked her to dance and picked Rigoberto. Maria says she picked Rigoberto because, "He was cute. He got my attention, and, he looked like he would be fun." They danced a few songs and went back to her table where he met her mom and sat down to talk with them.

During their conversation, he told them about another club he and his friend knew of in San Pedro, and asked them if they wanted to come along. By the end of the night, Rigoberto and Maria had set up another date for the following day, but Rigoberto had forgotten about it until his friend reminded him and gave him her address. When he arrived at her place to pick her up, she was outside. He asked if she was ready to go and she said, "Yes," and called her mom to come. Obviously, Rigoberto was surprised that her mom was going with them, but he didn't mind since he wanted to be with Maria.

"I want to spend the rest of my life with Rigoberto. It's been the best decision I've made in my life." —Maria

It only took a few days for Rigoberto to fall in love with Maria. He explained, "She was different from the other girls I had dated. Although she was only 19 at the time, she was very mature, and she was always looking forward to the future."

Shortly after they met, Maria would be leaving for Mexico on vacation. When she was away, she constantly thought of Rigoberto. They talked on the phone every weekend and wrote letters to each other. Maria was falling in love. She says, "Rigoberto made me happy when I was with him. I really liked the way he treated my mother, and she liked him a lot from the very beginning."

When she returned from Mexico, she could hardly wait to see Rigoberto. When they were together, they talked about getting married, and within six weeks from the day they met, they were husband and wife. Nine months later their first child was born.

"We have trust in each other because we've known each other for so long; we work as a team." —Rigoberto

Since Maria was more forward thinking than Rigoberto, she suggested they start saving to buy their own home so that their kids could grow up with enough room in their own home. Eight years and two kids later, they purchased their home.

Rigoberto says their marriage is successful because, "We don't take our marriage and life too seriously. We talk things over when we have problems in order to settle them; we keep a sense of humor, and always strive to be flexible." Maria says, "Marriage is a two-way street. We love and respect each other; we're always willing to work out our problems, and we know every problem we have or will come up can be fixed."

On their 25th wedding anniversary, Rigoberto took Maria and all the family from the United States back to Mexico so they could be married in a Catholic church with all their family, because he knew it's one thing that Maria always wanted.

Love, respect, and trust are the words that best describe their marriage. "Marriage has been the best thing that has happened for us," says Rigoberto. Maria says, "We've grown up together, and we've known each other for a long time."

Robert & Agatha Goodeau - Menifee, California
Married 34 Years - Anniversary: June 18, 1977

Robert and Agatha have been married for 34 years. When asked how they met, they each had a slightly different version. Both versions have them attending a Sly &The Family Stone concert at the Hollywood Bowl and then leaving the concert hand in hand. Agatha says she had been giving out wrong numbers all that day, but gave Robert the correct number. "Why I gave him the right phone number, I have no idea." Agatha was in high school when she met Robert. They dated three years before they were married. While dating, Agatha let Robert know that she could not be with him unless he had goals, a career, or something going on. She soon learned Robert had goals and desires, too--for himself and the two of them together. He was very determined to make a life with Agatha, so he left the state to learn a trade in order to better prepare himself to take care of the family he was now working towards creating.

"The Lord has blessed and honored our dreams and wishes of how we wanted our life and marriage to be." —Agatha

Graduation for Agatha came on June 15, 1977, she was married to Robert two days later; she was 17 and Robert was 22. Agatha's parents were not too excited about the news of their daughter getting married so soon after high school without attending college, but they were very supportive of their decisions. Robert's grandparents had met Agatha and had decided that she was going to be "the one."

After 34 years of marriage, Robert and Agatha admit it wasn't easy. In fact, they say it was a struggle and there are still challenges to get through. Getting married so young, they had to mature into the people they are today, while simultaneously having to work and raise their children. They both stress that they were able to make their marriage work, first because they loved each other. Additionally, they listened to each other, they treated each other as friends and they started early focusing on their goals and working hard together at making them happen.

They've had a variety of challenges, but like most marriages, finances play a big role. The money factor is huge especially when raising children, and dealing with their wants and needs. The couple learned over the years to put money away during the good times in order to get through the lean periods that were sure to come. "We continue to keep our finances in prayer. What we can't handle, we put in the Lord's hands," says Robert. As a result, they've been blessed with the family they set out to create from the beginning of their marriage. Outside of finances, there was the maturity issue; they were married very young, and there was a certain level of maturity that was necessary in order to make and ensure a successful marriage. Agatha adds, "I was still young and trying to mature and grow into being a wife, a mother, and a woman."

Robert and Agatha have raised two beautiful daughters who are on their own creating lives for themselves, and are assets to society. Agatha says she used to cry when their daughters left home, but now that they are grown, she loves when they visit but also loves the fact that they have their own lives. Now that the kids are gone, Robert and Agatha are able to go back to the way their lives were in the beginning, to the spontaneous dating, basically starting all over again. They've joined a wine club, take long drives, and go to concerts.

"We made a lot of mistakes along the way." —Robert

In their marriage, both Robert and Agatha agree that through it all, the love, the family support, and their commitment to each other have kept and continue to keep them strong as they listen to and understand each other, while remaining determined to make their marriage work.

Sander (Sandy) frequented the local Red Onion restaurant during his lunch breaks. At that time, Sandy was a police officer for the City of Manhattan Beach. He liked the fact that he could get his food quickly and get back to work. He went there so much they knew what he would order when he walked through the door.

This particular day, there was a new hostess, Roberta. He spoke to her as he walked in and noticed how nice and friendly she was. While eating, he spoke to the bus boy (Sandy knew everyone there); by the time he finished talking to the busboy, he had compiled all the information he needed regarding the new hostess.

Sandy finished lunch, went back to the police department, and called back to the restaurant. Roberta answered the phone and Sandy said, "Hi Roberta, it's Sandy, officer Rogoff. I was just there, and I was wondering if you date guys?" Roberta replied, "I think so." Sandy then asked, "Can I call you? I'd like to take you out?" Roberta said, "O.K." Just before Sandy hung up, he asked, "Would it be alright if I called you tonight?"

Roberta gave Sandy her phone number, and he called her later that night after work. They talked on the phone for more than an hour. Roberta was pleasantly surprised that he could keep the conversation going for as long as he had. She thought he was very interesting and intelligent. Sandy says Roberta was very attractive, fresh, and honest.

Sandy and Roberta dated off and on for the next two years. During their dating period, they broke up a few times. Roberta wanted to date other guys, but didn't find anyone out there that could compare to Sandy. Their last breakup lasted about two months; thereafter, Sandy brought some records by Roberta's place. The records were Sandy's excuse to see Roberta,

"Love, understanding, strength, and trust are words we use to describe our marriage." —Roberta

and as a result, they got back together.

Two years after they met, they were married. They both knew they were the right person for each other. Sandy says, "It makes me feel good to be good to Roberta and do things that make her happy. It's easy to be a loyal friend and warm to someone that is genuine and sincere."

"I had to watch less sports and give more attention to Roberta." —Sandy

Although Sandy and Roberta loved each other deeply, there were times when Roberta found it hard dealing with Sandy. Roberta explains, "Sandy was single for a long time and was set in his ways. He liked sports (a lot), and in the beginning it was the source of our bickering." During those times and a few others since their wedding, they've gone to marriage counseling for help. Sandy says in his defense, "I worked long hours; that, combined with the different situations I encountered on the job, I was exhausted by the time I got home, and I wanted to have some time and space to relax and unwind--and most times I'd do it in front of the tv." Sandy ends by saying, "I learned to watch less sports and give more attention to Roberta."

Roberta also realized that Sandy was a homebody. He was at home a lot even while watching sports. She knew where he was and was grateful for that, so she learned to like sports so she could be with him while he watched.

Roberta adds, "We've always had a natural attraction for each other, and that attraction is as strong today as it was in the beginning."

Sander Alan & Roberta Rogoff - Seal Beach, California
Married 35 Years - Anniversary: August 28, 1976

Charles & Darlene Dixon - Los Angeles, California

Married 36 Years - Anniversary: November 15, 1975

Charles and Darlene grew up within two blocks of each other in south central Los Angeles. They went to school together from grade school through high school, but they didn't begin dating until they were in their mid twenties. When they connected, Darlene was at Compton College watching the performance of an act she managed. During the performance, she kept seeing this guy in the audience wearing white pants with a pony tail, looking "real yummy" as she puts it. Later, while with a group of friends, someone said, "Darlene, this is Charles." Charles was that same yummy guy Darlene had seen during the day.

"Keep your marriage exciting to each other."
—Darlene

That was the beginning and they dated less than a year before getting married. Charles says, " I was too antsy, after 6 or 7 months, I'm thinking--what's happening, let's do this!"

Early on Charles never considered being married to Darlene for the remainder of his life. He says, "I thought she was fine, she cooked well, the sex was good, she was willing to take my s….t; I felt I could marry her, so let's do it before I change my mind."

The couple was married underneath a pryamid that Charles constructed in his studio, so that their union could not be broken by them, anyone, or anything.

Darlene's attraction to Charles was primarily due to his creativity, his kindness, his looks, his love, and a strong sexual attraction. "I loved his art, and I was overwhelmed by the respect he showed in his work for African American women." Charles says, "I've been practicing art since I was 12 years old. Art has always been my release valve, my salvation, and also my religion of sorts, because it has kept me prayerful and also humble."

"The way our realtionship lasts, is being receptive to change." —Charles

When asked what have been some of the challenges they've had to endure during their marriage, Charles answered, laughing, "Her opposite opinion!" After their laughter passes, Charles says, "The biggest challenge in our marital relationship is trying to keep an understanding of each of our points of view, while coming to a common ground and keep from having a breakdown in our communication."

Darlene interjects, "Being married to an artist is a challenge in itself. Anyone that has creativity flowing through them is not the 9 to 5 kinda person, so you gotta understand what that's about and let it flow into what it's going to be. To remedy those challenges, we have to maintain the magic we felt when we first met and fell in love. After a lot of years you can forget, and we need to keep that solid in our minds."

36 to 49 Years

Ye-pondering

if I could do 4ever
I think I might do it with you
4ever goes by
in the blink of an eye
and your way calls me forth to
I do

La Grande & Sonya both grew up in Southern California. Their parents knew each other before either of them were born. They grew up around each other because of their parents' longstanding friendship, but it wasn't until they met at church in their teens that they started to look at each other differently.

"A perfect marriage only exists on tv, and it only lasts for 30 minutes to an hour." —La Grande

La Grande is an only child, but he grew up with his twin cousins who were like brothers to him. Although these cousins would often tell Sonya that La Grande was interested in her, nothing came of it until the two of them were at a function with friends. Their other friends began to pair off, and since they were near each other, they started talking. La Grande says he knew that Sonya was the one. They then paired off and began talking at that function with their friends. It wasn't until a year later that they started to date. Sonya suspected that La Grande was the man for her early on as they dated, but she really *knew* two years into their relationship. At the time, La Grande was 17, and Sonya was 15 and in high school.

Although LaGrande and Sonya were in love and wanted to get married, Sonya was still in high school and wanted to go to college. They were married 2 weeks after Sonya graduated from high school. Their parents were concerned because they were so young, but they gave them their blessings. LaGrande's parents adored Sonya; she was the daughter they never had, and her parents loved him.

This couple explained that both their parents had long standing marriages and they were good role models for the way they wanted to conduct their marriage. LaGrande says, "Our parents truly loved each other; they romanced each other. Our fathers were gentlemen, they opened doors for their wives, they helped them in and out of the cars, took them out, and bought them gifts. They did those things because they truly loved their wives."

As she expressed her thoughts on why their marriage is successful, Sonya explained, "First and foremost is putting God first in our lives and trying to be obedient to His Word and live our lives according to His Word." La Grande added, "We like each other. Above and beyond the love and respect we have for each other, we're best friends. We have a lot of common interests, and we have the respect for space, time, and freedom we allow each other; and we don't smother each other. We have certain things each of us like to do separately and it's not a problem."

Romance keeps the Masons' marriage working. They set aside every Wednesday for their date night, and they do their very best to make sure nothing gets in their way of spending quality time together on that day. They also enjoy traveling together, getting away and being able to see something different other than the "same ole' walls" at home. La Grande says, "I still gotta be a Mack Daddy, and she's still gotta be a Hot Momma; that's what keeps us going! It's just that important. I still gotta bring it, especially if that makes her happy."

"Romance keeps the marriage working." —La Grande

The Masons sum up their 38 years of marriage thus far by saying, "Our marriage means a long lasting journey. We don't know when the end of that journey is going to be and we are grateful to God for the sights and scenes up to this point… and to have a traveling companion in each other, because it's that much more fun, interesting, and adventurous. So when the end comes, we may not know it; it will just end and we'll be on the other side, and we'll remember the wonderful times."

La Grande & Sonya Mason - Los Angeles, California

Married 38 Years - Anniversary: July 8, 1973

Johnny & Jeannie Zapara - Sacramento, California
Married 38 Years - Anniversary: August 19, 1973

Jeannie met Johnny through her brother, who was Johnny's college rommate. She was told that Johnny was "fabulous" and her brother wanted them to meet. They met when she was 17 years old, between her junior and senior year of high school. After high school, she enrolled at Christian Boarding College where she and Johnny met again.

They dated other people when Jeannie came to college, but as they attended social gatherings in groups, they began to enjoy each other's company more and more. As they got to know each other better, they both realized they were more interested in each other than the people they were dating.

When they began dating, it never dawned upon either of them that they wanted to spend their lives with each other. They were simply enjoying each other's company and having a good time together while learning to honor and respect one another. After about a year of dating, Johnny and Jeannie broke up. After the breakup, and considering the possibility of losing her forever, Johnny realized that Jeannie was exactly the kind of person he wanted to marry.

Although Johnny and Jeannie were no longer a couple, her brother asked Johnny to look after her while he was away in the Army. They were still at the same college, and they began to talk again. Over a period of a few months, they decided to get back together and get serious. Shortly afterwards, they were engaged. They were married approximately five months later.

"Before we got married, I said, 'If this is possible, this is what I want to do: are you willing to commit with me that we will not fight?'" —Johnny

The Zapara's credit their success in marriage to their strong faith in Jesus, because Jesus has been the center of their marriage from day one. In college, Johnny had a professor who announced to the class that he and his wife had been married for 36 years and had never had a fight. After class, Johnny spoke to him about it and decided that if Jeannie was in agreement, they would make a commitment that they would not fight either. Their commitment was tested numerous times in the first few years, but they persisted, if for no better reason than to keep a record going. After a while, it became second nature. "We disagree... maybe there are times our feelings get hurt, but we've never shouted at each other, called each other names, walked out, or had a marital fight," Johnny says.

"The other thing that has kept our marriage really good is the fact that we like each other; we love each other, but we like each other also. We enjoy being together." —Jeannie

Although Johnny and Jeannie were committed to no fighting in their marriage from the beginning, there has been a bigger challenge to the success of their marriage. The Zapara's went through a major spiritual change in their marriage early on. Thirty years ago, they made a decision to leave the demoninational structure that they had been a part of for three generations. It was a pretty tight knit religious structure, but they came to the conclusion that they could not stay there. They admit that, "Making that decision and growing into that conclusion and the process simultaneously was very challenging, but we were committed to doing it together without fighting about it or over it."

To help maintain communication and connection within their marriage, the Zapara's strive to maintain a habit of retreating to their family room early in the morning where they spend 30 to 40 minutes together and separately with the Bible. They pray together aloud, pray for each other, their children, work days, and things they have in common. They stay up to date with each other through prayer, talking, more prayer, and more talking.

Robert and Rosie Davis grew up in Monroeville, Alabama. They met at a birthday party where Rosie made such an impression on Robert that he went to her home the following Sunday morning to ask her parents for permission to "court" her, as they did in those days. Rosie was at church when he came to visit. According to Mr. Davis, their meeting was basically "love at first sight." They agree about this, because during their dating process they were separated for almost 2 years, yet got back together and were married shortly afterward.

"The Bible states the man should be the head, but if there is no one to help direct that head, that head could get out of control." —Rev. Davis

Prior to their marriage and before Mr. Davis became a minister, he and Rosie were out on a date with another couple when he had a terrible accident. Mr. Davis had been drinking and had been driving too fast. He, Rosie, and the other couple walked away from the accident without a scratch. That night, as he dozed off to sleep, a vision of his deceased grandfather appeared to him in a dream. These occurrences, along with the fact that after he attended a Christian tent service with his mother and father, his parents say while driving home, he preached to them the entire distance. Mr. Davis doesn't remember any of this.

Mr. Davis does remember driving Rosie to her parents' house and saying, "I must preach. Do you think we can make it with me preaching? Rosie's answer was, "Yes."
Rosie had been going to church but had not fully accepted Christ, but Mr. Davis says, "With me preaching, she came to the Lord and accepted him in her life." They wed two years after meeting.

Both Mr. and Mrs. Davis come from homes where their parents maintained long lasting marriages. Mrs. Davis says, "Our parents' marriages were inspirations to us. When we began our union, we had witnessed the trials and tribulations they went through, watched them work things out, and that gave us reason to believe we could have a successful long lasting marriage also.

Mrs. Davis says, "Communication is the key to a successful marriage. Whether you are pleased or displeased with your spouse, talking the situation through to its end is a must." Mr. Davis adds, "Trust, along with communication helps a marriage to become successful, because once trust is lost, the marriage is on its way to dissolution. And during trials and tribulations, before the communication can begin, there has to be time for the healing process to begin."

"Our marriage is successful," says Rev. Davis, "because we trust each other. We communicate our likes, dislikes, and most importantly we trust in the Lord. We put Him first because He guides our path.

Rev. Davis says, "We have our ups and downs just like anyone else. An older minister years ago said to me, 'Where ever you go, whatever is going on at home between you and your wife, when you get out in public, you and your wife need to be the ideal couple, because you are looked upon for guidance; and if you appear to have things out of place in your life, you won't be of any help or inspiration to others.'"

"Marriage has to be a joint effort, and you should strive to do it together." —Mrs. Davis

Rev. Davis has been doing premarital counseling for couples for more than 30 years. He says while in class with one of his mentors, he learned from him that he counsels couples in 15 minutes instead of the 4 to 6 weeks that other ministers were accustomed to doing. He says he asks the couple four questions. If the answer to any one of the questions is a "no," he says he tells them they are not ready to get married. The four questions are: "Are either of you willing to *stop*, *start*, *give*, and *take*?" According to Rev. Davis, "Before you get married, you have to have made up your mind to *stop* doing some of the things you were doing before you were married, *start* doing some things you were not doing before you got married, be willing to start *taking* some things you were not before you got married.

Robert & Rosie Davis - Monroeville, Alabama

Married 39 Years - Anniversary: July 1, 1972

Donald (Donny) had just been discharged from serving his country in the Vietnam war when he attended the Watts Writers Workshop in Los Angeles with his best friend, who was acting with Patricia in a play. He says Patricia was butting in when he was having a conversation with someone. Since Donny was newly discharged, he was still in uniform as he hadn't had time to buy civilian clothes. Patrica made it clear that she was against the war. Needless to say, they didn't talk too much at that meeting, because of her outspoken opposition of the war.

"Our marriage has been a growing process."
—Donny

The next time they met, they were at a cast party. This time Donny was not in uniform and there was no talk of the war. During this meeting, they decided that they liked each other. They didn't date until a few months later because of their schedules; she was busy with the Writers Workshop, and he was busy working two jobs and getting his life together.

Their first date was at Disneyland because Patricia's father was a postal worker and the families of postal workers could attend. After the first date, Patricia said, "Donny, for some reason, I have this feeling that you are going to be somewhere in my life for a long time." Since that first date, they've been like best friends, doing all kinds of things together and just hanging out. Patricia says, "Donny could make me laugh. We could talk to each other."

Pat knew Donny was the one for her because of his relationship with his family, and how he interacted with his brothers, sisters, and friends. The first positive thing about Patricia as far as Donny was concerned, was that she didn't have any kids. She had high standards, good morals, and she could communicate well.

Donny and Patricia dated two years before they were married. Patricia says she planned on marrying *once*. And she had made up her mind

that she was going to work at their marriage and work out situations that came up so that they'd have a successful marriage.

Early on in the marriage, Donny admits that he "did knuckle head things." He says, "I've learned to be a better husband because I continue to tell mysef to do better. I tell myself all the time, *just shut up,*' because my mouth is my biggest problem." Donny comments that, "When I started to go to church, I saw how other men treat their wives, and I began to learn from watching them." After Donny and Patricia were married, he still wanted to go to nightclubs, but Pat didn't go because she stayed with the kids. Pat let Donny know that it was not a good idea to continue to go to clubs, because things could happen if he kept putting himself in that atmosphere. Donny thought about the situation and what effect it could have on his home and marital life, and conseqently, he stopped going out unless Patricia was with him.

"Donny and I have made an agreement to never go to bed angry. We attempt to resolve conflicts before we go to bed. Once resolved, we never bring the situation up again."

"If I hadn't gotten married, I'd be dead. I was going no where fast! —Donny

Donny and Pat Turner both agree that their marriage is successful because they've worked together over the years. They have a great respect for each other, and in addition to liking each other, they are in love with each other.

Patricia says, "A husband and wife can't be just lovers, they have to look upon each other with pride, and both have to have integrity. Our marriage means we're following a convenant that God set and it's not to be broken; we're in alignment with the way God wanted our lives to be lived."

Donald & Patricia Turner - Bellflower, California

Married 40 Years - Anniversary: March 21, 1971

Hank and Faya met in 1965 while attending a summer school program at Harvard University. Hank was in an Arts and Sciences program and Faya Rose was in a law program.

Being African Americans in a predominately white environment at Harvard, they were naturally drawn to each other. They learned they both had roots in Alabama and came to refer to each other as "home people." They spent some time together that summer, but they later formed a strong friendship during their last two years of college after Faya enrolled at Harvard full time, and Hank joined her there a year later. Faya says, "We were really close as friends. Hank was probably the closest friend I had. He was the person I could talk to. I had always been the person that gave advice, or provided a shoulder for people to cry on."

Faya graduated a year before Hank and decided to visit him in his home city of Bay Minette, Alabama. She had secured a job in Oakland, California in legal services and was on her way there when she went to visit Hank. During that trip, their relationship moved from being just friends to dating, and because of that change in their relationship, Faya Rose decided to take a job in New York so they could be closer together as Hank finished college.

"Intimacy is the glue that holds relationships together through the rocky times." —Faya Rose

Hank and Faya's relationship was born in the heat of the Black Power Movement; the "Black is beautiful" and "Love my Black Man" movement. "We formed our relationship in an era when people were re-affirming the positive traits in Black men and women, and black male and female relationships," says Faya.

Five months following the move to New York, they decided to get married without inviting their parents or friends, they became husband and wife. Faya explains, "I don't think I was really ready for a real serious relationship at the time, but you can't time things like that; and Hank is not the kind of person to sit around and wait for me to make up my mind." Hank adds, "We both realized that marriage is a struggle, but it's worth the struggle. Once you understand it's going to be a struggle and it's worth it, you put in the effort to make it work.

"There is a freedom in our marriage for each of us to pursue our own mission." —Hank

"Strong marriages are based on strong relationships, and they have to be deeply rooted in something that is concrete, not just *infatuations and sexual desires*. Our marriage is successful because we started our relationship with a deep friendship that was based on respect and love for each other as human beings. On the other side of that, we are very different people, but we have the same vision, the same goals, and the same mission. We have different ways of reaching that mission, but we each have respect for our differences."

Hank and Faya have been working together in their law office and in the community for more than 35 years. "We both travel frequently and stay very busy but there is no jealousy between us because one is waiting at home while the other is away," explains Hank.

Faya says, "We are patient with each other. In a marriage, we each have to figure out what we can tolerate or put up with that doesn't go against our core values and principles."

"When you look at a person and 90 percent of what they do is positive and contributes to your welfare and happiness, you can get off track by that last 10 percent, because it comes from the fact that we are not perfect people," says Hank.

Henry (Hank) Sanders & Faya Rose Toure - Selma, Alabama

Married 41 Years - Anniversary: January 23, 1970

Jay and Sue Ahrend have been happily married for 41 years. They are a very creative couple; Jay is a semi-retired professional commercial and advertising photographer, and Sue is a practicing ceramic tile artist. They met at a pool party for the attendants of a wedding that they were both involved with. They took an immediate liking for each other and began dating the very next day. By the time the wedding occurred, they had spent every day together following their initial meeting at the pool party.

Jay was finishing his studies in photography at the Art Center in Pasadena, California. Sue had already graduated, but had always wanted to take classes at the Art Center. She had a great appreciation and respect for Jay's attendance there. The course work at Art Center was very demanding of Jay's time and energy, but the two of them were able to continue to successfully date through the remainder of Jay's study there. According to Jay, "A lot of art students had relationships when they began their studies at the Art Center, but as time passed, they were no longer in those relationships, because the college was so demanding. Sue understood those demands and was accepting and accustomed to the situation, because she was also an artist."

Jay and Sue spent the next two years getting to know each other, and since both of them were artists, they enjoyed doing many of the same things. Their creative sides gave them lots to talk about: things like art, photography, and her tile work. They also shared many of the same core values; their religions were similar, and they came from similiar family backgrounds—both their parents maintained long standing marriages. They also had the same number of siblings. Sue had one brother, and Jay had one sister—whose name was Sue.

"In any relatlionship, you have to learn to accept the person you're with for the person they are, and not the person you want them to be."
—Sue

Jay says of his proposal to Sue, "I asked her what she was doing this coming summer, and before I could finish, she jumped up and started swinging around the apartment saying, "I'm getting married, I'm getting married!!" Jay says he was a starving art student, so "there was no big drawn out occasion with a big diamond ring, roses, nor a down-on-one-knee event." Jay and Sue were married 2 years from the day they first met.

"Marriage makes us stop being selfsh and learn about our spouse; it's not just all about you. You learn commitment, sharing, and responsibility."
—Sue

Jay explains, "Our marriage is successful because we don't compete with each other for friends or time. We support each other's ideas and concepts in each of our careers, and we don't try to dominate each other." Sue adds, "If there is a disagreement, we compromise or we give in to each other once in a while; but one person does not always win. There's always a give and take—our entire relationship can be based on that." The couple agrees that their marriage has not had any challenges that threatened their union. "Our marriage is so natural for us, we don't have to work at being happy together," says Jay. But they confess that life has, indeed, thrown them some curves that they've had to work together to get through.

One such challenge presented itself to the couple after Jay underwent surgery, and the medicine prescribed to him caused a personality change. They realized that they had to work this out somehow, so they decided to give each other the floor to air their grievances while the other had to listen. Sue said, "We sounded off, and we had to be respectful of each other's point of view, especially if that point of view was very different." Sue explains, "In any relationship, you have to learn to accept the person you're with for the person they are, and not the person you want them to be. You have to let people work things out in their way, and let them be who they are."

Justus (Jay) & Sue Ahrend - Long Beach, California
Married 41 Years - Anniversary: June 6, 1970

Rohn and Jane met at Hope College, a Christian College in Holland, Michigan. Jane was in a sorority and Rohn was a member of their brother fraternity. They met during the last six weeks of their senior year. After graduation, Jane came to Rohn's house in Grand Rapids, Michigan for a few weeks during the summer. Rohn gave her a ring and asked her to be his wife. They were employed in different states and didn't see each other again until Easter of that year.

Having a long distance relationship required Rohn and Jane to spend a lot of time talking on the phone and writing to each other; they also recorded cassette tapes to mail to each other. Getting to know each other well enough to get married took appoximately 10 weeks from the date they first met. According to Jane, "I knew he would be a good husband and father, and would take leadership in the family. All the things I thought a Christian marriage would be, I saw in Rohn. He came from a very stable Christian family and that was very attractive to me." "Knowing Jane loved the Lord is probably the element that was in the backgound the whole time; it's probably the number one reason we are married to this day," explains Rohn.

After Rohn and Jane were married, they were separated because Jane was working in Yorba Linda, California and Rohn was working back East. Rohn eventually became a teaching Vice Principal of a Christian school in Santa Rosa, California, where they were together in one place.

"Marriage is probably the biggest transition anyone will go through in their lives." —Rohn

This couple spent the following years getting to know each other as they learned to live together, and to start their working lives and family. Jane said, "The first ten years of marriage you're still trying to make your spouse like yourself. You marry him because of the opposite attraction, but then when you get married, you try very hard to make him just like you." After taking her marital concerns to the Lord, Jane says, "God said He was my husband, so I said, 'Well Lord, if you are my husband, what do I do with him?' and He said, 'Enjoy him!!!'" Jane and Rohn are not shy about going to God with their concerns.

The Ritzemas' have had, and continue to have, challenges in life, although they don't let these challenges threaten their marriage. Jane explains, "Running to the Lord as often as I need to, helps to make our marriage successful. I've done it so often I have calouses on my knees."

"There have been many times our wedding vows have kept us committed." —Rohn

When Jane was 40, she had a miscarriage; her mother had a brain operation that left her an invalid; and she was diagnosed with breast cancer. All of this happened 6 months apart. Jane again went onto calloused knees to the Lord to voice her concerns. According to Jane, "God healed me. He said, 'Jane, I don't want you to have a broken a broken body. My body has been broken for you.'"

Not too long afterwards, Rohn had 2 heart attacks; then he was diagnosed with cancer also. After putting off surgery as long as possible, Rohn gave in and sought out professional help, and the doctors were able to remove all of the cancer.

Rohn explains, "There have been many times our wedding vows and our faith in God have kept us committed. Often the thought comes to me, 'For better or worse, in good times and bad, in sickness or in health, til death do us part.' We continue to hit hard places in our lives but we continue to take our concerns to the Lord. Marriage is a forever covenant…sometimes it means being out of control."

Rohn & Jane Ritzema - Elk Grove, California

Married 41 Years - Anniversary: June 29, 1970

John and Verla Saylor are sitting in the serenity room in their 1918 craftsman style home in Long Beach, California, where they've lived for the the past 35 years.

They've been married for 42 years. When they met, both of them were married. Verla had 3 teenaged boys, while John had a teenaged daughter.

Verla's friend told her about an opening at John's medical practice for part time help. She learned that along with her pay as an employee, she would also receive free medical benefits for her family. She took the job right away.

"We've had more fun than most millionaires..." —John

At the office, they had become a great team, because John didn't like doing anything except taking care of the patients, while Verla took care of everything else that happened in the office.

John likes to say that when Verla would drive him to various hospitals for his rounds, he'd get out of the car and say, "Thank you." Verla would reply, "The pleasure is all mine." He knew then that she was the person he wanted to spend the remainder of his life with. Verla says, "I knew John was the person I wanted to marry when he accepted my teenaged sons along with me. He said, 'I welcome the responsibility.'"

Interacting with each others kids was a major concern in the beginning, because Verla had teenaged sons and John had a teenaged daughter. After a while, though, that was not a major concern, because John treated Verla's sons as if they were his own, and through the years, they've done lots of fun things together.

Their problems during their marriage have been no greater than "Spilled milk." During each dinner, one of the teenaged sons would

spill a large glass of milk. "We don't have a failure to communicate, but sometimes it gets loud," says Verla.

John and Verla were married on July 29,1969, in the chapel at Long Beach Memorial Hospital during John's rounds at the hospital. They traveled to Japan for their honeymoon.

As a medical doctor with his own practice and Verla as a nurse, John, along with a partner, was able to create a schedule that consisted of 5 days on and 5 days off, which allowed them plenty of time to travel throughout the states and abroad.

They took great pleasure in traveling all over the world after they were married. While their kids were teenagers, they traveled with them. As the kids grew up, John and Verla would take trips alone. They once rented a vehicle in Europe and drove through 28 countries in as many days. Since they've been married, they've had lots of laughs and adventures together. "We both love to laugh. We'd sacrifice anything for humor," says Verla. John and Verla Saylor have been retired since 2000. John retired from his medical practice at age 80 after 50 years of practice.

"We both love to laugh. We'd sacrifice anything for humor." —Verla

They still enjoy their time together, but they don't suffer for lack of space. John screens independent movies several times a month, and Verla plays bridge once or twice a week. They both feel it's important to have separate activities. Even though they spend time away from each other, they continue to communicate as if they were together. When John has a break between movies, he calls Verla and tells her about the movie he just watched.

John and Verla continue to live the creative, interesting life they started together 42 years ago.

John & Verla Saylor - Long Beach, California
Married 42 Years - Anniversary: July 29, 1969

One afternoon Rudy and Mariana played together in the front yard of Mariana's aunt's house in Buenos Aries, Argentina; they were ten years old then. After that day, they didn't see each other again for 20 years when Mariana came to Los Angeles, California for a visit. Rudy and Mariana's mothers went to school together and grew up in the same neighborhood in Argentina. Their grandparents knew each other also, as they came from a tight knit family community.

Mariana was visiting her brother in the United States and decided to end her trip with a two week visit in California. Since her mother knew Rudy's mother, she stayed with them when she visited Los Angeles. Rudy was her tour guide when she came to visit. They spent a lot of time together and found they had a lot in common. They came from similar family structures. They also liked the same kind of music and the outdoors. They both had a love of travel, because each of them had traveled extensively throughout Europe.

As Mariana prepared to leave, Rudy gave her an engagement ring and asked her to marry him. Rudy had fallen in love with Mariana during her ten-day visit. When asked how he knew she was the one, he said, "I can't explain it, I just knew she was the one. We felt the same about so many things, and we were very comfortable together." He also says, "We were both almost 30 years old, and we had done the things we wanted to do as singles. We were mature, and we knew we would have a successful marriage."

Mariana traveled back to her home in Buenos Aries to make preparations for the wedding. They decided to have their wedding in Argentina since most of their friends and family still lived there. The wedding ceremony was performed in church and the reception was at Mariana's house.

They honeymooned in a resort town about 500 miles south of Buenos Aries called Mar Del Plata.

After the honemoon, arrangements were made to move Mariana back to Los Angeles where they began their life as a married couple. Mariana says, "We began with very little; we didn't have any furniture in our apartment, our first table was an orange crate which the neighbor downstairs had thrown out." Rudy adds, "You start there and you make whatever you earn last, and the next year gets better, then the next year is even better. Then you can buy some of those things you want; it all comes from working together."

"Our goal is to make this marriage last." — *Rudy*

"We've never had a problem of spending too much money. If anything, we spent too little," says Rudy. "I was in the habit, maybe from my dad, of putting half of whatever I made in the bank and the rest I have to learn to live with. If I didn't have enough, that's too bad! The money that's in the bank has to stay there and grow. That's what my dad drilled into me; you gotta have it because there will come a time you'll want a new car or something. He said 'don't go into debt, that's the worst thing you can do.'"

Our marriage has lasted because we both work at making it last. Rudy says, "I want to remain married to Mariana for the rest of my life. A little bit of luck, a lot of patience, and a lot of love. Mix it together and that's the glue that holds our marriage together."

Rudy & Mariana Heske - Los Angeles, California

Married 42 Years - Anniversary: November 9, 1968

Kenneth Lee & Christina Lynn Green - Lakewood, California

Married 43 Years - Anniversary: October 7, 1968

Ken and Chris met at Douglas Aircraft Company in Long Beach, California. They were not yet 20 years old. Ken operated a blueprint machine and Chris delivered blueprints throughout the facility. The company was so large that she and a few other women made their deliveries on roller skates. Ken worked there for a year until he was drafted into the military. He spent 2 years in South East Asia as a Marine before returning to work at Douglas Aircraft. Chris didn't think much of Ken after he came back to the company, because he started at a higher level than some of the other workers who had been there longer. After she learned that his advancement over the others was because of his service to his country, she viewed him differently.

As time passed, Chris would skate by Ken's work area just to see him, even when there were no blueprints to be picked up. Although Ken had noticed Chris's outfits as she skated around, he didn't make any advancements towards her, because he thought she was dating a friend of his there at the job.

"We are not just a married couple, we are best friends." —Chris

Chris was wondering why Ken hadn't seemed to notice her, nor had he said anything to her, so she asked a friend about him. One day while the three of them were standing around in Ken's work area, this friend said, "Ken, why haven't you noticed Chris and said something to her?" Ken was caught off guard and couldn't say anything. Chris was so embarrassed that she immediately skated away.

A few days later, when Ken and Chris met in the hall, she let him know that she was a little angry because he had never talked to her. Ken explained himself, and as a result of that meeting, they made a date right then. After the first date, they learned that they liked doing a lot of the same things and had a lot in common. Following that first date, they spent quite a bit of time together getting to know each other. They would get together before and after work and on weekends with family. Chris was very much in love with Ken and hoped he felt the

same about her. During a conversation with Chris, Ken asked: "Do you think you could spend the rest of your life with me?" She answered, "Are you asking me to marry you?!" "Yeah," Ken responded. Chris' reply to his proposal, of course, was "Yes!" A month before he proposed, she had been feeling like he was the one she wanted to spend the rest of her life with. Ken proposed around Valentine's Day, and approximately nine months later, they were married.

One of the challenges they've had to deal with as a married couple came when their first born son was about 18 months old. They found out that he was born with a cataract on one of his eyes. This was a very difficult time in their marriage. Chris wondered, as any mother would, if there was something that she could have done and didn't, and about the care that she was given during her pregnancy. Working together with their son in his growth and development and talking things out, they were able to work through this first major hurdle as well as other challenges over the course of their 40-plus years of marriage.

"Ken has always been my rock." —Chris

The Greens also learned early on—the hard way—about managing their finances. The unnecessary use of credit cards taught them that if they didn't really need the item they were charging, they could live without it until they could afford to pay cash for it, especially if that purchase was going to cause a lot of stress and bickering in the relationship. They managed to live by that principle, and sticking with it over the years has proven to be very successful financially. Plus, it has helped to create a successful marriage. Ken advises: "Make your mate the focal point of your whole life. If you treat them the way you want to be treated, all other problems will seem minor. If you love them, you'll treat them with that love and respect that you want. Love them and the love will come back."

The Greens describe their marriage as "happy" because of the stability, longevity, and comfort they've established and share together as a couple.

Stanley & Dorthy Burstein - Los Alamitos, California

Married 45 Years - Anniversary: August 14, 1966

Stanley Burstein was in his third year of studies at UCLA when he noticed Dorothy (a freshman) in his Latin class. "I thought she was attractive and I wanted to get to know her," recalls Stanley. He asked Dorothy to have coffee with him. She accepted and they began having coffee every day. It took Stanley a little while before he asked her out on an official date, but when he did, Dorothy was not able to accept. She didn't tell Stanley that she couldn't go out with him because she had dates lined up for the next couple of weekends!

"You make a point of not demanding what the other person can't give." —Stanley

They continued joining each other for coffee and were getting to know each other better. When they were able to go on their first date, they went to the Mardi Gras held on UCLA's campus. During their date, they stopped by a marriage booth, got married (unofficially), and walked away with their certificate. They had lots of fun that night. After that date, Dorothy determined that Stanley was more interesting than the others she had dated, so she began seeing him exclusively.

Dorothy says she hadn't thought much about marrying Stanley until her cousin asked, "Is he the marrying kind?" Dorothy answered, "Yes," although she and Stanley didn't talk about marriage until much later.

When Stanley's mother met Dorothy for the first time, she asked, "Are you serious?" Dorothy thought his mother was a little forward, but she answered yes to her question. Later, Stanley's mother helped to push the issue by announcing her newfound interest in diamonds.

Stanley and Dorothy were sitting in the back of a shuttle bus on their way to the parking structure to pick up their car when Stanley announced, "I found a diamond; would you be interested?" This was Stanley's way of asking Dorothy to marry him. Dorothy was interested, so she answered, "Yes."

Stanley wanted to get married, but because he and Dorothy were still in college, he knew that he could not support a wife. They decided to wait until after they both graduated to get married. As they discussed marriage, they talked about having children. Dorothy wanted to have children, but Stanley wasn't sure. It was very important to Dorothy, so she said, "No children, no marriage." Stanley wanted to have Dorothy as his wife, so he agreed to them having children. According to Dorothy, "Stanley went from not wanting children to being a wonderful father."

Shortly after they were married, their first child was born. They decided that Dorothy would take some time off from work to raise their child. They would have to make it on a professor's salary, which was not much then, so they went through some economic difficulties. Dorothy says she didn't buy clothes for 5 years. During the years she was off work, she went back to college for an advanced degree. When she went back into the work place, she earned double her previous salary and more than Stanley.

"Getting along with a person for 45 years is an accomplishment in itself!" —Dorothy

Both Stanley's and Dorothy's parents came from the depression era and lived accordingly. Stanley and Dorothy didn't have any money problems aside from the 5 years when Dorothy was not working and was home raising their child. Stanley says, " We've always had enough money, not rich, but we've never had to worry about those issues since neither of us have extravagant tastes and lifestyles, and we've never spent too much. The only good financial decision I've made was marrying Dorothy!"

Dorothy says their marriage is successful because, "We treat each other properly, we respect each other, and we indulge whatever quirkiness we each have." Stanley smiles and admits, "I feel happy if I walk into a room and she's there!"

Alberto & Zita Revilla - Burbank, California

Married 46 Years - Anniversary: June 18, 1965

Alberto and Zita are both from Peru. They met through friends in Lima where they were pursuing an art education. Alberto was studying sculpture, and Zita had just finished high school and was studying painting. They were both in their late teens. As they spent more time together, they developed a great respect for, and trust in each other.

Five years had passed when Alberto asked Zita to become his wife. Before that, Zita had not thought much about marriage; she was more concerned about completing her education. She accepted Alberto's proposal and they were married in Peru. Shortly afterwards, however, Alberto purchased a visa for five dollars and traveled to the United States to seek better employment opportunities in the arts. He was in the United States just about a year before he sent for his new bride.

"We did everything as a family; that's another reason our marriage lasted as long as it has." —Zita

Zita joined him in the U.S.A. where they would start their lives together. "Just after I arrived from Peru, Alberto said to me, 'When you are upset about something, I'll be quiet, and when I'm upset about something, you be quiet; that way we won't argue.'" Zita laughs and says, "When I was upset, Alberto would always be quiet, but I never would. I'd keep talking and talking, so he would go to his workshop in the garage."

Life was not so easy as Alberto sought employment in their new country. The first two years were the toughest as he worked diligently to maintain life and his new marriage. After being in the United States for 3 years, Alberto and Zita were able to buy their first home. They lived there approximately 20 years as they raised their two daughters. During those times, Alberto worked a full time job to take care of the household needs and a part time job to make sure they could send their two daughters to the best schools they could afford.

Zita says, "We were very good friends before we got married; maybe

that's why we are still married—that, along with the fact that Alberto spends a lot of time in the garage working on his sculpture, while I handle things in the house. During those years, we had nothing. Our house was bare, but we didn't worry about that because we were all together, and we were happy. When we could afford the material things in the house, we would save our money and buy them."

The couple says that another reason for their long lasting marriage is the fact that they did everything as a family. There were hardly times when Alberto wanted to do things without them; everywhere they went, they went as a family. Zita loves that Alberto is a very quiet and patient man. She says it made it very pleasant being with him as they raised their kids. One of the toughest times in their marriage was when they, as a family, went to Peru for a visit. Alberto and Zita were told they could have residency in the U.S. and Peru at the same time. Their daughters were born in the U.S.A., so they were going to make them Peruvian citizens, but the paperwork was not completed before it was time for them to leave. They were unable to leave because of the laws in Peru. Alberto had to get back to America in order to go to work, but everyone else had to stay. They were eventually able to get the correct papers filed through Immigration and get back to the U.S. If they had stayed one more week, the girls would not have been able to come back with them. Zita has not been back to Peru since.

"We were very good friends before we got married; maybe that's why we are still married." —Zita

Alberto is now retired. He and Zita spend their time with their daughters, the grandkids, and with each other going to the movies, galleries, and museums. Alberto still spends quite a bit of time in his garage workshop doing sculpture, while Zita keeps busy in the house. Now, instead of using the string with a bell on the end of it to communicate between the house and garage, they now use their cell phones.

Sam & Ella Mae Sanders - McDonough, Georgia
Married 47 Years - Anniversary: May 1, 1964

Sam is the eldest of 13 children, and Ella Mae is the youngest of 12. They were both born in the 1940's in Bay Minette, Alabama. Both their parents maintained long standing marriages, as it was uncommon to hear of very many divorces during those times. Their families were not financially well off and they worked hard for everything they had.

"Marriage is different from dating. When you're dating, you go home at night, but when you're married, you're there 24-7." —Ella Mae

Sam and Ella Mae grew up in the same area, and attended the same schools, but it wasn't until Ella Mae's last year in high school that they began dating. Ella Mae recalled that, "I knew just after I finished high school that Sam was the man I wanted to spend the remainder of my life with. We always knew we would get married."

When asked how she knew Sam was the man for her she said, "We had those special feelings for each other and I knew that Sam was a hard worker. Although we didn't start with anything, I knew that together with Sam and his work ethic, we could have anything we wanted".

After high school, Ella Mae went to California to visit her brother, while Sam headed to New York to work and go to school. Although there were miles between the two of them, they stayed connected through letters and phone calls. Ella Mae was in California for about a year when she returned to Alabama. Her next stop would be Connecticut, and from there her final destination would be New York where Sam was now living and working. Over the miles and the passage of approximately three years since they met, their love brought them back together where they still remain.

Sam and Ella Mae paid for their own small wedding in New York. There were no delusions of grandeur, because as Ella Mae puts it, "We've known each other most of our lives; we weren't raised with money, and since we'd never had money, we knew when we got married we would have to work for everything we wanted."

They were married for four years before they started having kids. They wanted to spend time with each other, because they knew when they began having children, their lives would change, causing them to focus their attention on the kids and less on themselves.

Respect and constant communication are the cornerstones that have made and keep Sam and Ella Mae's marriage successful. Ella Mae said, "After marriage, we had to get accustomed to respecting each other as a married couple and being able to know what each of us required in the marriage." Sam added, " At this point in our marriage, we know what each of us wants, so we try to make sure those things are at the top of our list as we go about our day-to-day activities."

"We accept each other for our own separate personalities." —Sam

Through the years, Sam and Ella Mae have gone through their ups and downs, including the pride of purchasing their first home. In addition, they've shared the joys of bringing their three kids into this world and raising them in a way that would cause them to be assets to society.

Their honesty with each other, their respect for each other, and the communication they've shared over the years has led to 47 years of lasting love.

Robert & Marlene Sherins - Pacific Palisades, California

Married 48 Years - Anniversary: July 21, 1962

Robert and Marlene were introduced to each other by Robert's new roommates. He had just moved to an older home that was being rented to a group of medical students who worked with him at the same medical center. Marlene remembers driving up to this house and having the funniest feeling that the man she was going to marry lived there.

Since they lived in the same house, their paths crossed daily. One day Robert asked Marlene out on a date. Marlene says that when they were dating, it was not always a Saturday night date where he'd see her all dressed up. She says, "Sometimes he'd see me in the morning with my hair in rollers, or going to the market, or vacuuming and cleaning up. Our encounters on a day-to-day basis were more realistic; he was able to see me as I am. He had a very real and honest view of me as opposed to only seeing me pretty for a Saturday night date." The couple agree that their relationship evolved steadily from comfort, to trust, to friendship. Marlene states, "You become friends, underlying everything else based on your values and interests." Both Robert and Marlene had the same values, even though they were raised in families with different religions.

"I always thought marriage should last for a lifetime..." —Marlene

As they dated, they reached a comfort level--the atmosphere between them was relaxed as they grew and were able to fill a certain space in each other's life. It was approximately 9 months into the relationship that they began to talk about marriage. Robert's family is Jewish while Marlene's family is Catholic and Protestant. "We had to deal with how our parents and friends felt about it," Robert says. "My parents thought I was very fortunate to have chosen Marlene for a wife."

Bob and Marlene had very little money in the beginning since they were both attending college, but they managed. Thankfully, they did not have an exaggerated appetite for consumption. Neither of them ever had credit card debt, no expensive club memberships, or children wasting money; as a result, they were able to curb costs. Their only debt has been the mortgage on their home and the cost of setting up Robert's medical practice.

When asked what has made their marriage successful, Robert responded with, "I don't think either of us would say that we sat down and deliberately analyzed the relationship, the reason, or the basis. From where we came, divorce was not common in either of our families.

"To be comfortable with yourself, you have to know who you are." —Robert

We were stable from the beginning, and we were grown-ups, we matured earlier than most, and were much more self reliant and responsible for ourselves. The idea that we were responsible for the marriage was really secondary only to being responsible for the professional goal: to get through the schooling to do what's necessary, stick it out through very difficult schooling, because as one would imagine, medical school is very difficult. It takes a lot of preserverance, so early on we decided to be supportive of each other through the hardships." "I always thought marriage should last for a lifetime, because the world and families need stability, and it seemed like a natural thing to stay together. And unless something is radically wrong with your partner, you should stick it out," commented Marlene.

"In our marriage, besides being in a loving relationship that brings about a certain level of stability in our lives, it's nice to have a safe haven within a successful marriage." says, Marlene.

Jim and Mary Beth Heglund grew up in the small Midwest city of Red-wig, Minnesota. They met in Jr. High School in the 8th grade. They played together and went to school and church together. Their parents were good friends before Jim and Mary Beth were married. Their marriage of 49 years is a perfect example of two people being familiar and comfortable with each other. Growing up together was the perfect opportunity for them to get to know each other. Additionally, being from a small city with families that were very similar was also another plus for them. They inherited their value system from their parents and were able to look at their successful marriage as a starting point for their own. Mary Beth says, "We came from a generation where you just made it (marriage) work; things evolved, we took things easy, letting life happen."

"It's nice that we like the same things, because agreement comes easily for us." —Jim

While in Junior High School, Mary Beth asked Jim to what is called a "Sadie Hawkins dance"—it's when the girls ask the boys to a dance; that's when the friendship began. They became close friends, because as Jim explains, "We got along well, and we had fun together." Jim and Mary Beth continued to get to know each other throughout their remaining years in school together. After high school, they enrolled in the same college. After graduating from college, they were married, and a few months later moved to Southern California after being recruited for teaching positions. They said they were only going to stay a year, but they've been in California since 1962. Jim and Mary Beth both confess that their move made them so much more independent.

The Heglund's agree that their marriage is successful because there is a lot of give and take, and they've been able to gracefully do that. Jim jokingly admits, "I always give in to her. We share responsibility for everything—child care, finances, work, and cooking; but with that sharing, we usually come out doing the things we like." Mary Beth says, "Jim likes to cook, but I don't; he's a very good cook. We also talk about things, and we let each other be ourselves."

Jim and Mary Beth have gone through many challenges, just as most married couples do, but their challenges have never been with their marriage or their relationship with each other. Neither of them have had any major health issues, but their most difficult challenges have been of a medical nature with their two sons as they were growing up. "Our biggest concern was our kids' health and well being," says Mary Beth. They say they were able to get through those difficult periods and others by supporting each other. Each of them would put in well over 50% by picking up where ever they were needed. "Those kind of things were done because of our love for each other; and sometimes just being there helps out a lot," says Jim.

The Heglund's built a friendship that started in their preteens and it is still growing and lasting through their 49 years of marriage. Mary Beth says, "Marriage means security, and having a good friend. We like the same things--classical music, we're opera buffs, and we share a lot of the same interests. We are also different, and differences are good; but at the same time, we are not that different. It's a blessing to be able to share every day with someone you love; you're not alone or lonely."

"Our religious faith has been a big part of our marriage." —Mary Beth

Jim & Mary Beth Heglund - Northridge, California

Married 48 Years - Anniversary: August 11, 1962

Willie & Bettye Williamson - Long Beach, California/Summit, North Carolina

Married 48 Years - Anniversary: September 23, 1962

Bettye was a senior at Polytechic High School in Long Beach, California when she and Willie met at a taco stand after a night of skating at the now defunct Pike Amusement Park in downtown Long Beach. Willie had recently moved to Long Beach from North Carolina. He was sitting in his 1954 Mercury with a close family friend of Bettye's when she stopped to talk and was introduced to Willie. Before they met, Willie had gone to some of Poly's football games that season and had seen Bettye there. He liked the fact that she was outgoing and very outspoken. After seeing her at some of the games, he decided he'd like to meet her, but he had no idea he was going to meet her that night.

Some time after they met, Bettye and a few of her friends were going to a Café in San Pedro, California, when they saw Willie driving near them. They got his attention and he followed them to the Café. They talked there, and shortly afterwards Willie took her to a few football games. In those days, there weren't a lot of places to go on dates like clubs and other adult places, because Bettye was only 17 and still in high school. So they'd see each other, talk on the phone, and cruise around town in Willie's car. They were able to get to know each other little by little.

"We make decisons together; if it's a bad decision, we made it together." —Willie

Willie took Bettye to her senior prom, and it was during that time that Bettye says she thought Willie would be a good husband for her. They continued to date after Bettye graduated high school. As Willie worked to establish himself, he wasn't having much success, so he decided to go back to North Carolina. While he was away, he and Bettye continued to communicate by calling and writing each other. They both realized that although they were apart, they had developed deep feelings for each other. Nearly six months had passed before Willie came back to Long Beach to be with Bettye, and approximately 3 years after they met, they were married.

The first years of the Williamsons' marriage was tough as they worked to get a handle on their finances. Three years into their marriage they gave birth to their daughter, Kesha. Willie and Bettye's break came a little more than seven years into their marriage. During their early years of marriage, it was difficult to find gainful employment, but eventually, they both were fortunate enough to find well paying, lasting employment. Shortly after they changed jobs, they were able to purchase their first home.

"I think your husband needs to be your best friend." —Bettye

Since the major challenges and difficulties in their marriage amounted to no more than getting control of their finances, the Williamsons were on their way to a loving, lasting marriage. They attribute the success in their marriage during those trying times to having faith in God, patience with life and each other, and being able to talk through situations that have come up over the years. Bettye says, "I think you have to have God in your life; that's very important to us. Our marriage is based on our faith in God, faith in each other, love, respect, and most of all, we are each other's best friend.

Some of the most memorable moments in their marriage include the birth of their daughter, purchasing their first home, traveling together, and they recently have been blessed to be together to see their daughter give birth to their first grandchild.

Willie and Bettye are retired and spend 6 months of the year in California and the remaining 6 months in Norh Carolina or other travel destinations. Travel is one of the ways they keep their marriage exciting. Willie says, "We love traveling together, because we like to be together and around each other." Depending on the destination, they travel by motor coach, cruise ships, or airplane. Over the years and since retirement, they've visited most of the 50 states and Canada. They've taken cruises and traveled abroad together. Willie explains, "It seems like I've been married so long, I wouldn't know how to act not being married, because I love being married to my wife."

Always & ForEver Love

50 to 73 Years

Be Still Mine Heart

I woke this morning
next to you

recalling my concerns
my fears
my reserve

your very smile
whispered

silent simmerings
that tugged @ my heart
to remembering

what a difference a day makes
with great joy does our love ache

© ImmoBme az.i.B.we (Laura Cook)
Jan. 10, 2011

Fred & Lurlean Towns - Inglewood, California

Married 50 Years - Anniversary: March 19, 1961

Fred and Lurlean both have 12 siblings. Lurlean is the oldest of her family: 11 girls and two boys. They lived in the neighboring towns of Hainsville and Homer, Louisiana. Fred's brother was going to see one of Lurlean's sisters, so he went along because he was told there were a lot of sisters. Fred and Lurlean met that night but didn't see much of each other until they ran into each other at Southern University in Louisiana where they both attended. They would see each other around campus and at dances. As they talked, they learned that they had a lot of similarities when it came to family values, principles, and family upbringing.

"Blessed is the best word to describe our marriage." —Lurlean

After college, Fred moved to Farmington, New Mexico to look for work, as he had family there. Like most small towns during that time period, there was little gainful employment available.

Lurlean was still in college, but they communicated by calling and writing. They learned a lot about each other over the distance and found that they wanted to see each other more. Their long distance relationship lasted about two years when they started talking about a long term relationship and marriage. Fred and Lurlean were married in March of 1961, just a few months after Lurlean graduated from college. They had a simple wedding at Fred's mother's house in Hainsville with family and close friends.

By the time they were married, Fred had moved to Los Angeles, California for better job opportunities, and to be near family. A few days after their wedding, Lurlean packed up her belongings and drove to Los Angeles with her new husband. They lived with Fred's sister for a few months when a cousin sold them their first house in East Los Angeles.

Shortly after purchasing their first home, they started their family. Lurlean stayed home to raise the children while Fred worked as many jobs as he could to provide for the family. As the children grew older, Lurlean began working as a school teacher to help with the financial responsibilities that come with three growing children, a mortgage, and other obligations.

As things improved financially, Fred and Lurlean were able to purchase a motor home so they could travel together as a family. "Traveling by motor home has been one of the best things we've done as a family," says Fred. "It keeps us all together, and that's very important to us."

The children are now grown with their own families, and Fred and Lurlean have retired but they still travel by motor home. "Traveling to different places for weeks and sometimes months together helps to keep us excited about having the time to spend with each other in our retirement," says Lurlean.

The couple explains that travel, either in the motor home, by plane or cruises to the Islands, Hawaii, Mexico, Alaska, and other destinations, has been the source of major highlights in their marriage.

Fred and Lurlean give credit to their faith in God for the marriage they've built over the 50 years they've been together. "We've remained faithful and loyal to one another and put God first on our priority," Lurlean says. "Next, we try to keep each other next to God on that list, and we pray a lot seeking God's word for guidance. We believe this has helped us to stand the test of time."

"We've remained faithful and loyal to one another and put God first on our priority." —Lurlean

McKinley & Gola Dailey - Atmore, Alabama

Married 51 Years - Anniversary: August 27, 1960

McKinley and Gola came from large families. Both their parents had long standing marriages, although Gola's parents passed away at a young age. Watching their parents interact together gave them both a good starting point for their marriage. Gola says, "My mother let me know that marriage was not always going to be a smooth road." Both she and McKinley felt it was important for their kids to see them interact in various circumstances.

McKinley and Gola met at a mutual friend's home in Atmore, Alabama. They began dating in Pensacola, Florida, where Gola had moved and McKinley was attending college. They both admit that at the time, they were not thinking about the other being the one they would marry and spend the remainder of their lives with. They say they developed a mutual interest in each other, and as they got to know each other they fell in love, so the next step was to get married. They knew each other about a year before they were wed. McKinley said, "Once I got to know her and continued to see her, I fell for her." Gola says, "McKinley is humble, sweet; he's loving and very kind, which made me love him more."

Gola said there were times during their marriage when they could have given up and gone their separate ways. They were able to work things out because they wanted to make sure their kids were taken care of; but most of all, their love for each other was the glue that held them together during those rough times. McKinley advises, "The both of you have to know what your problems are and be able to work through them together." McKinley was saved, and shortly thereafter Gola followed. They both agree that was the turning point in their marriage, because it was then that they realized what marriage was all about. "Knowing the Word of God lets you know that when you take your vows, it's serious," McKinley says. "From that point on, we put God as the Head in our lives. If you have Christ in your life, you'll have guidance and you'll be led in the right direction."

"My mother let me know that marriage was not always going to be a smooth road." — *Gola*

The Daileys say that being able to do things together, and being able to laugh together and laugh at each other helps to keep the excitement alive in their marriage. McKinley explained, "We went on vacation every year when the kids were little; it helped the marriage and helped the children to grow." Now that the kids are grown with their own kids, McKinley and Gola enjoy traveling together to see them because it allows them time to spend with each other.

"Once I got to know her and continued to see her, I fell for her." —*McKinley*

Communication, trust, love, understanding, and forgiveness are things the Daileys say have made their marriage successful for the past 49 years.

Harold and Mary Williams met at a jook joint in Freemanville, Alabama as teenagers. Mary's parents were friends with the owner of the jook joint, and when she visited she brought Mary and her sisters along with her. Harold says, "I thought she was about one of the prettiest things that walked the streets. She was as pretty as a speckled puppy!"

Both Harold and Mary grew up in church. Harold would travel to McCullough where Mary lived to visit her and attend church with her. They spent the next 3 years getting to know each other. When they were married, Mary was 19 years old and Harold was 20. Mary says that she knew that Harold was the person she wanted to spend the rest of her life with because: "I've always been a religious person, and once I married one time, if I find the person I love, that would be it for me."

"I thought she was about one of the prettiest things that walked the streets. She was as pretty as a speckled puppy!" —Harold

When Harold and Mary were married, their finances were not the best. Even though they both worked, they still didn't have much money. To make matters worse, they began to have children shortly after they wed. The next three years brought them three children. They waited three years before they had their fourth child. Taking care of 4 children and building a house at the same time was not easy, but they made it through.

Financial challenges improved as Harold was able to make more money, but things made another turn for the worse after the first child

graduated from high school and went to college. For the next two years, two more children graduated from high school and went off to college. Now, there were three kids in college at the same time, with one left in high school. Finances remained tight until all the kids had graduated from college.

"I've always been a religious person, and once I married one time, if I find the person I love, that would be it for me." —Mary

As each child was accepted into college, Harold and Mary helped them pack their belongings and drove them to their colleges. They drove to Tampa Florida, Philadelphia, and the University of Alabama.

During high school, Harold and Mary's daughter played on the girls' basketball team, while their two sons played on the football team. They attended all the games, both at home and away. They both look back on those times as some of the best in their marriage, because they were traveling together as a family and spending time with each other as a couple. They learned how to talk to each other and to compromise during those long drives to and from games.

Family was most important to the Williamses. They acknowledge that putting God first, loving and raising their children, loving and trusting each other, and being involved in their kids' activities helped to keep them focused on staying together for the sake of the family as a whole. Mr. Williams says, "When you have children, if you love the wife, you'll love the children."

Harold & Mary Williams - Freemanville, Alabama
Married 51 Years - Anniversary: January 2, 1960

Johns & Ange'le Sumi - Redondo Beach, California
Married 52 Years - Anniversary: August 29, 1959

During the summer of 1959, both Johns and Ange'le were traveling from Europe to America. Johns traveled alone, bound for New York to further his education as a dental technician. Ange'le first visited the United States in 1957. It was during that trip that she fell in love with New York City and decided that she wanted to live there. She and her brother were going to New York to live with her aunt and uncle. Ange'le had no plans of returning to Europe.

"Be good to the family and take care of the children... We are family people." —Johns

Speaking of her marriage to Johns, Ange'le said, "It was meant to be!" She remembers them meeting on the ship and spending time together: "We'd see each other just about every day; we took pictures together, and saw each other during the day and at dinner. My brother and Johns both loved playing ping pong, and they played the game together during the trip." Upon arrival in New York, they went their separate ways, but Ange'le gave Johns the phone number to her aunt's house. Johns called a few days later to let her know that he had the photos from the ship. Ange'le thought it was an excuse to see her, but she was okay with it because she knew that Johns was in New York alone, so she agreed to see him. They began spending time together, often going to the beach. Since neither of them knew very many people in New York, they spent as much time as possible getting to know each other better, despite the language barrier. Ange'le spoke French while Johns spoke Armenian. In order to communicate better, they both spoke French, and eventually they began communicating in English only.

Their attraction for each other was so strong that after a few months of getting to know each other, they decided to take a chance on marriage. They both believed even if people have known each other for a long time, they are still taking a chance on marriage. Although they hadn't known each other for very long, their thought was, "When you marry, you marry for life." Johns and Ange'le came from households where their parents were married only once. Johns and Ange'le were married on August 29, 1959. They had a small wedding in a Catholic church in Brooklyn, New York, with about 20 people in attendance.

The Sumi's started their family one year after they were married. Ange'le remembered that in the beginning of their marriage, things were difficult because they had limited financial resources. In addition, they had no family nearby to help them with the children, plus, they were burdened with any number of other obligations. Johns and Ange'le explained that in New York in the late 50's, finding a place to live and work was not a problem, so because they were able to find employment and an apartment right away, they were able to get a good start.

Being on the same page financially has been a great asset for the Sumi's. From the very beginning, they were never materialistic when it came to their style of living. Mrs. Sumi says, "You have to save, save, and save… We started out saving $10.00 a week…I've saved for so long, now I don't know how to spend, because I've saved for so long." Since their lives were not based on material possessions, the Sumi's were able to do the things they loved to do together, especially travel. They recalled lots of stories of their travels together and as a family.

"Marriage has given us more patience and understanding for each other." —Ange'le

When asked what makes their marriage successful, after a few moments of thought, Ange'le says, "I don't know how we did it!" Johns added, "You get used to each other; after so long, you know each other's weak points and you just get used to it." She adds, "We've both grown and changed together, and we met in the middle."

Taking a chance on marriage has proven very successful for the Sumi's, because they are still in love with each other after having been happily married for 52 years. Ange'le mentioned, "Our marriage has made us better together. We enjoy our life together, the children, and grandchildren…We have a nice, simple, happy life!"

Walker & Lillie Peoples - Freemanville, Alabama

Married 53 Years - Anniversary: June 14, 1958

Walker and Lillie met when they were about 14 or 15 years old in the small town of Atmore, Alabama where they lived. Their family backgrounds of growing up on a farm were similar, which gave them a place of reference and a starting point. Since most people in the town (Blacks and Whites) knew each other, it was easy for them to get to know each other, especially since they attended the same school. Although they grew up together, they were not allowed to date until they turned 16. From their first meeting and thereafter, it seemed as if they were joined at the hip, because they were always together in their thoughts and actions.

When they were married at the age of 21, Lillie and Walker made a promise to each other that they would agree to agree with each other one way or another and try to keep the obstacles out of the way. They both agreed that they would leave their small home town, because they planned to have kids, and they would need to provide for them. Had they remained in the town where they grew up, their kids would have more than likely followed in their footsteps, which meant field work or farming, since those were among the few work options available to Black folk during those times.

"We've loved and respected each other from the very beginning." —Lillie

After moving to Tampa, Florida, the couple's lives really began coming together; they found a church home, they were both working, and were eventually able to buy a home to start their family.

The couple raised four sons and were able to put them through college, guaranteeing them a better life than they would have had if they remained in their small home town. They credit watching their sons grow into productive, successful young men as being one of the many highlights of their married life. "We lived for the kids, their school, college, and church activities," says Walker." They've had at least two of their four sons in college at the same time, which stretched their funds to their limits. During those times, they would pray about it and

Walker would go out on the weekend after working all week and do odd jobs to help make up the difference.

"Life itself is like this great big puzzle, and you're always looking for that missing piece, and until you find that piece that is missing, something is wrong..." —Lillie

Walker and Lillie say that in a successful marriage "You gotta have a made-up mind, trust, discipline, love, and you must keep others out of your marriage." Lillie says, "We've loved and respected each other from the very beginning." To have longevity in a marriage, you must have two people who trust and respect each other, otherwise you won't make it.

Lillie recalls that her mother told her, "I want you to realize that you are supposed to be the wife, mother, housekeeper, caregiver, and all that…. Once you start doubting that, things will break down. It does not hurt to be friends with people, laugh and talk, help people, but keep them women out of your house, because when you see too many women crowded up together, it's just about to be a problem there. When you see that one or two of them is there to cause that problem, you gotta know how to guide yourself through it and keep it from coming in." Lillie says, "I live by what my mama taught me."

"I took my wedding vows very seriously," Lillie adds. "The Bible tells us that once you come together and say 'I Do,' it's no more two people, you become one, and I've always tried to live by that.

Throughout your marriage, you got to put GOD in it; without Him, none of us is anything. It took prayer for us to make it this far. We spent a lot of time praying! I always told GOD, the devil will always have to get behind me, walk beside me, get under me, but he was not going to get in front."

Mr. and Mrs. Lambert have known each for most of their lives. They both grew up in Atmore, Alabama, and met when Eddie was visiting Katie's church. He was 15 and she was 13. They became fast friends and, eventually, high school sweethearts.

Since they met in church, it's easy to see why after more than fifty years of marriage, Eddie and Katie are very spiritually grounded and still very active in their church. The church gave them a solid foundation on how to live their lives and how to treat each other.

Katie liked the way she was being treated by Eddie, and based on that, she knew he would be a good husband and father.

Their love and respect for each other grew through getting to know each other as children in church and watching each other grow up. Both came from large families that had long standing marriages, so it was only natural that they attempt to emulate their parents when it came to marriage.

After knowing each other for about 7 years, Katie and Eddie were married. Their marriage produced 4 children. Mrs. Lambert was a stay-at-home mother until the kids were in school, after which she went to work also. Her husband took care of the household expenses while she bought the extras for the house and kids.

"Everything we have is ours together. There is no such thing as mine or his; it's all ours. Togetherness is the key. Togetherness is what keeps you together," says Mrs. Lambert.

"I haven't always been good." —Eddie

As with most marriages, there are good times and bad times, but their bad times were not enough to end their marriage. Mr. Lambert says, "I haven't always been good. I did some things that if I could turn back the hands of time would not have happened. My Momma said, 'Sometimes you go over fools hill and do things that are not pleasing to a marriage.'"

"Sometimes you go over 'fools hill' and do things that are not pleasing to a marriage." —Eddie

Eddie also added, "I've made some bad choices in my life, but you're supposed to learn from your mistakes and ask for forgiveness. If you mean to do right and do the right thing, marriage is not that hard."

Eddie & Katie Lambert - Atmore, Alabama

Married 56 Years - Anniversary: June 4, 1955

Robert & Marjorie Hubert - Whittier, California
Married 58 Years - Anniversary: November 22, 1952

During the Korean War, Robert was in the Navy on an oiler. They were coming back into the Navy Ship Yard in Long Beach, California, when he learned that his first wife was divorcing him. He was in pretty bad shape for about two months because of it, but while in Long Beach, he was talked into going ashore for a dance.

"Marriage means I'm still loved and someone will love me whether I make sense or not." —Marjorie

Marjorie was working in downtown Long Beach at a bank where she was asked to be a hostess at the same dance that Robert was going to attend. Marjorie had also been married and divorced. It was 1952, and there weren't many divorces in those days. Robert reluctantly attended the party, but to his surprise, a young lady there caught his eye. (This young lady, of course, was Marjorie.) He immediately went over and asked her to dance. He and Marjorie spent the remainder of the night talking and getting to know each other. In fact, he felt more at ease with Marjorie than he did during all the years with his first wife.

The following day, Robert and Marjorie went on their first date. They spent the whole day together. The next day, he left on the Navy ship heading for Japan. He was gone for 6 months, but he and Marjorie were in constant contact through letters they wrote to each other. Through their correspondence, they were able to get to know each other very well. In one of the letters where they spoke of getting married, Marjorie wrote, "I can't cook; I'm not a good housekeeper. All I want to do is love you, have your children, and be your wife." Robert's response in his return letter was, "I don't care if you can't cook. I don't care if you can't clean house; I just want you to be my wife and have my children."

Robert came back to Long Beach in June 1952 after being discharged from the Navy, and he sent for his mother to come to meet Marjorie. They all got along well as they toured Los Angeles and the surrounding areas. After his discharge, Robert was unemployed with no place to live in Long Beach, and that led to him having second thoughts about

marriage. But he remembered all the things he liked about Majorie and what he had gotten to know about her over the past six months; plus, his mother loved her.

Robert and Majorie were married on November 22, 1952. Robert went back to college, attained his degree and began teaching high school in Long Beach. He was very active at school outside of his classes. He and Majorie spent lots of weekends at high school games and functions. Marjorie stated, "It got to the point that I'd either have to watch the games with him or I don't do anything with him." They lived comfortably with their two children on Robert's teacher's salary. Robert knew he would never get rich on a teacher's salary so they lived within their budge. They didn't have credit cards, and they spent wisely. He'd get a raise each year and that made things manageable as the years went by.

Robert said, "Our marriage was successful because we respected each other; we put each other first. We had God's help, and you can't get any better help than that. We were secure in our marriage because we had love, trust, security, faith in each other and in a Higher Being."

"You don't plan for yourself, you plan for each other." —Robert

At the time of this interview, both Robert and Marjorie were in their mid-80's. They still went on dates. Each day they would drive to the local Weinersnitzel for lunch where they would sit and talk and watch the kids getting out of school.

Robert and Marjorie met January 30, 1952; on that same day in 2010, Marjorie Huber passed on. She will be missed by all who knew her, but she will be missed most of all by Robert Hubert, the love of her life.

Robert said in the interview, "We're both approaching our last years together and I don't know what I'd do if I survived her."

Walter & Thelma Pratt - Austell, Georgia
Married 58 Years - Anniversary: August 1, 1952

Walter Pratt and a friend were leaving church one Sunday when he saw Thelma and her friend Mildred walking along the street. The year was 1946, and the city was Atlanta, GA. Thelma and her friend were on their way to a nearby neighborhood called "Summer Hill" to visit an aunt. Walter and Thelma talked for a few minutes, and that was enough to leave an impression on him.

"Working together makes our marriage successful." —Thelma

The 1940's were tough times for colored people, or Negroes as they were referred to in those days. They lived in the "Alley" or the "Rear" of Atlanta. These were the days when a lot of people didn't have electricity, automobiles, or telephones.

Walter found out where Thelma lived and stopped by unannounced for a visit. It took a few tries to catch her at home because she had several jobs and was attending night school. Thelma eventually had to quit night school. Being the second oldest of 17 siblings, she had to put education on hold to help support the family.

Walter—or Pratt, as Thelma calls him—began spending a lot of his free time with Thelma. Their thinking, goals, and desires were along the same lines. They both came from poor families, so they knew they'd have to work very hard for everything they attained. "Pratt and I wanted to have something because we were both born poor. People around us tried to make us feel that we could not do better than we were doing. We've always had it in our minds that we wanted to do better than our parents did," adds Thelma.

Pratt grew up in Oraville, Alabama where he learned farming. He brought his knowledge of farming to Atlanta with him where he and Thelma began farming together from the time they met. They both agree that farming and "working together" at any job that provided an honest income outside of their regular jobs has helped to maintain and keep their marriage successful.

Pratt and Thelma knew each other 6 years before they were married. After they were married, they rented a room in a tenement house from a friend of Pratt's until they were able to purchase land to farm and build their own home. Their working relationships with their employers helped to make it possible for them to purchase land and make payments.

The couple has always passed their abundance in blessings back to those in greater need than they were. Since the beginning, they've always given the first farming crop away, along with meat from a packing plant where Pratt worked to help the elderly, sick, single mothers, and the poor.

The toughest times they've experienced were financial, because they wanted to secure their seven children's future. They raised them with the determined goal in mind that their children would have better opportunities and a better life than they did.

"God took care of us and we took care of our children." —Thelma

Both Walter and Thelma Pratt agree that farming has been one of the best things they've done together that has helped maintain their marriage since they met. Farming has kept them working together as a team and because they've always taken their children to work and farm with them, it's kept them together as a family. As a result, they've been able to feed their family, other families in need, and remain in love with each other over the past 58 years.

Jethro and Lizzie Mae met on a Saturday evening as they were going downtown (Atmore) to see a movie. Lizzie was about 15 at the time and Jethro was about 20. They both came from large families where their parents remained married until their deaths. Jethro and Lizzie's courtship lasted approximately two years before they were married September 21, 1947. Lizzie Mae says, "I thought about how I wanted to live, and I always said I wanted to be married to one man. I wanted all my children's father to be the same, and I didn't want to be separated." When asked how she knew Jethro was the person she wanted to spend her life with, she replied, "I thought he was the one because of the time we spent together; I got to know him, and he seemed like he would be a good husband and father." Jethro said, "She was the one I wanted. I really didn't think about how long it was going to last."

This couple says that their marriage has been successful because there has been a lot of give and take along the way. According to Mrs. Dailey, "Everything is not going to go your way all the time; you have to learn to work it out, and along the way, you just have to live with some things."

"There were times where we both have had to give in to the other to keep our marriage working." —Jethro

Mr. And Mrs. Dailey give God the credit for helping to guide them through the sixty-plus years they've been married. They say, "The Lord was with us all along the way. He made it plain in a lot of ways where our help was coming from. We look back and think about the things we didn't have and how we were able to get them, and we knew it was all His doing."

Mr. Daily said, "Reading and studying the Bible, along with going to church, teaches you right from wrong, so we try to follow that from day to day. We've learned to work together, cooperate with each other and help each other." He added, "In the lean times of our marriage, we learned to accept what we got and make good with it, knowing that the Lord will help us through."

"We had to work out how we were going to make it with the amount of money we had." —Lizzie Mae

Mrs. Dailey says that money has always been a struggle for them. "We had to work out how we were going to make it with the amount of money we had, and how it was going to take care of the number of children we had." In financial matters, the Dailey's continued to exercise their method of give and take. They would discuss what needed to be done to resolve a financial dilemma, and when they both agreed, they would proceed accordingly. Mrs. Dailey states, "We also learned to tithe. I believe you can have a little more when you tithe. It didn't seem like it would work like that with the little money we had, but we seem to have made it."

Lizzie Mae tells of one instance when her first daughter was in college: "She'd send home for money, for tuition or some bill or another, and sometimes we'd have only a few hundred dollars in the bank. The bill would be $500, and we'd wonder where we were going to get the money. Out of the clear blue sky, we'd receive a check in the mail for $500. It was the work of the Lord!!"

According to Lizzie, "We've been able to stay together all these years by managing to work things out and by trying to reach an agreement, and most of all with God's help."

Jethro & Lizzie Mae Dailey - Freemanville, Alabama
Married 64 Years - Anniversary: September 21, 1947

Willie & Eliza James -Tensaw, Alabama
Married 73 Years - Anniversary: September 29, 1938

Willie James is 102 years old, and his bride of 73 years, Eliza Mae, is 95. He was born in Blackshear, Alabama, and his wife Eliza was born in neighboring Clark County. It stands to reason why being in a marriage of such length leaves little to be said in regards to what it took to get there, because it's so comfortable, this couple cannot think of life being any other way. Willie can remember a lot of things about his life and the people in his life over the past 102 years, but he and his wife are a little fuzzy on exact time lines and events in their marriage over the years.

Willie was in his late twenties when he asked Eliza (22) to marry him in 1937. They were married at their local church. In those days for couples like Willie and Eliza Mae, there was no grand honeymoon after the wedding; once married, they quickly began the task of making a living and life together.

"I had in mind 'I love him', and I thought I should spend my life with him." —Eliza Mae

After their wedding, they lived in a Pole House (Log Home) that Eliza's father built. Willie worked different jobs during their marriage to take care of Eliza while she stayed at home and worked the farm. Willie says, "I always kept a good job, and never worried about money." Willie has worked in the saw mills, on tug boats on the Alabama river; he's logged in the Alabama woods, and helped to black top (pave) Highway 59.

Although Willie and Eliza Mae were going about life, living during early Jim Crow Laws and sharecropping, their most pleasant memories are from their married life together and the good times they spent making a living and raising their family.

This couple never had any really big fights, but when they had disagreements, they said they talked the situation over and came to a conclusion. Eliza said, "Marriage is like the weather, some good days, some bad." They added that being Christians and their strong belief in the Bible helped them live a loving life, so they tried to treat each other right. Willie says, "Marriage is a good life if you make it that way."

Both Willie and Eliza Mae have been retired for quite some time. Willie has farmed for most of his life. After retirement, his farming was mostly for his and Eliza's needs and to keep busy. Whatever he grew beyond their needs he gave away. Approximately 5 years ago, he stopped farming altogether. Now, he and Eliza spend all their days together.

When asked if they were still in love, Eliza Mae said, "I reckon so." She asked Willie if he still loved her. He said, "You know I do." She then asked why, and he said, "Cause you my wife." As if that was more than enough reason to love her. When asked the same question she said, "Cause he's my husband, and he takes care of me."

"Treat each other right." —Willie